Bourgeois Christians

Bourgeois Christians

Worldly Evangelicals and the Paradoxes of Paganism

C. Ashley Royal

FOREWORD BY
J. Aaron Simmons

WIPF & STOCK · Eugene, Oregon

BOURGEOIS CHRISTIANS
Worldly Evangelicals and the Paradoxes of Paganism

Copyright © 2025 C. Ashley Royal. All rights reserved. Except for brief quotations in critical publications or reviews, no part of this book may be reproduced in any manner without prior written permission from the publisher. Write: Permissions, Wipf and Stock Publishers, 199 W. 8th Ave., Suite 3, Eugene, OR 97401.

Wipf & Stock
An Imprint of Wipf and Stock Publishers
199 W. 8th Ave., Suite 3
Eugene, OR 97401

www.wipfandstock.com

PAPERBACK ISBN: 979-8-3852-3575-9
HARDCOVER ISBN: 979-8-3852-3576-6
EBOOK ISBN: 979-8-3852-3577-3

VERSION NUMBER 01/13/25

Unless otherwise indicated, Scripture quotations are taken from the (NASB®) New American Standard Bible®, copyright © 2020 by the Lockman Foundation. Used by permission. All rights reserved. lockman.org.

Scripture quotations marked (KJV) are taken from the Authorized (King James) Version. Rights in the Authorized Version in the United Kingdom are vested in the Crown. Reproduced by permission of the Crown's patentee, Cambridge University Press.

Scripture quotations marked (NIV) are taken from the Holy Bible, New International Version®, NIV®. Copyright © 1973, 1978, 1984, 2011 by Biblica, Inc.™ Used by permission of Zondervan. All rights reserved worldwide. www.zondervan.com. The "NIV" and "New International Version" are trademarks registered in the United States Patent and Trademark Office by Biblica, Inc.™

Scripture quotations marked (ESV) are from the ESV® Bible (The Holy Bible, English Standard Version®), copyright© 2001 by Crossway Bibles, a publishing ministry of Good News Publishers. Used by permission. All rights reserved.

For my grandchildren:

Holden, Tucker, Charlie, Amelia, Steve-O,
Jack, Jesse, David, Linley, and Caleb

that they may all grow to love and serve God

Reasoning and education, though we are willing to put our trust in them, can hardly be powerful enough to lead us to action. —Michel de Montaigne, *Essays*

Great learning and great shallowness go together very well under one hat.—Friedrich Nietzsche, *The Use and Abuse of History*

Now an Excellence of Understanding is not that which makes one Man more acceptable to God than another, even tho he shou'd employ it faithfully to the finding out the Truth, but the good Will and sincere Intention of applying one's utmost Forces and Facultys to the finding out and practising what God requires of us.—Pierre Bayle, *A Philosophical Commentary on These Words of the Gospel, Luke 14:23, "Compel Them to Come In, That My House May Be Full"*

It is through my body that I understand other people, just as it is through my body that I perceive things.—Maurice Merleau-Ponty, *Phenomenology of Perception*

For you have been bought with a price; therefore glorify God in your body. (1 Cor 6:20)

It is most shocking that someone can know everything and not have made a beginning on the least thing.—Søren Kierkegaard, *Three Discourses on Imagined Occasions*

For the kingdom of God does not consist in words, but in power. (1 Cor 4:20)

God grant the philosopher insight into what lies in front of everyone's eyes.—Ludwig Wittgenstein, *Culture and Value*

We are destroying speculations and every lofty thing raised up against the knowledge of God, and we are taking every thought captive to the obedience of Christ. (2 Cor 10:5)

Contents

Foreword by J. Aaron Simmons | ix
Acknowledgments | xiii
Abbreviations | xiv

Introduction and Description of My Method | 1

Chapter 1   Democratic Culture: Democracy as Equality of Conditions | 17

Chapter 2   Democracy in America Revisited: Habits of the Heart | 30

Chapter 3   The Therapeutic Culture: The Age of Self-Fulfillment, Sickness, and the Psyche | 38

Chapter 4   Evangelical Populism and the Thin Theology of American Revivalism | 48

Chapter 5   The Intellectualist Way of Being a Christian | 61

Chapter 6   The Cartesian Elements of the Cartesian Consciousness | 70

Chapter 7   Kierkegaard on Subjectivity and Nietzsche on the Emptiness of the Age | 79

Chapter 8   The Centrality of the Heart | 87

Chapter 9   Seeing-as-Understanding versus Hearing-then-Doing | 94

Chapter 10 The Truth Is *Aletheia* | 103

Chapter 11 Problems with a System—Even a Good One | 114

Chapter 12 Problems with a System—Captive to a System | 125

Chapter 13 Christian Ethics: From the Beginning to the End | 131

Chapter 14 Conclusion: The Quotidian Christians | 138

Bibliography | 143
Author Index | 151
Subject Index | 153

Foreword

J. Aaron Simmons

THE POSTMODERN PHILOSOPHER JACQUES Derrida once commented that he was perplexed that his philosophy was being embraced in evangelical churches (or at least by folks raised in such churches). I think his confusion at this fact was that his philosophy was so deeply critical of the doctrinal rigidity frequently found in such communities that ignores the complexity of hermeneutics, the play of language, and the contingency of social structures. However, if we pay attention to the way that Derrida helps us rethink the "idols" of our own making that serve to condition our norms, our practices, and our beliefs, then it would not be too perverse to suggest that Derrida might help churches remember what matters most about Christianity. Indeed, like Kierkegaard before him, Derrida, and other broadly existential philosophers and theologians such as Simone Weil, Dietrich Bonhoeffer, and Martin Luther King Jr., all call in question anything that goes under the name "Christian" that has become complacent and self-protective. I think we can rightly see all these thinkers as engaging in an "attack," to borrow from Kierkegaard, whereby the goal is to bring "Christianity back to Christendom." I consider Ashley Royal's new book, *Bourgeois Christians: Worldly Evangelicals and the Paradoxes of Paganism*, to be another text in this esteemed tradition.

Now, let me be clear, this is not simply one more book in the how-to-pull-the-church-back-from-its-cultural-captivity-in-postmodern-culture subgenre. Indeed, as a postmodern philosopher, I have read entirely too many of those sorts of books and found nearly none of them to offer anything even approaching substantive philosophical analysis. Alternatively, neither is this book an Evangelical-meets-postmodernism-

and-they-live-happily-ever-after sort of text. I am a Pentecostal Christian and so, perhaps unsurprisingly, I have read plenty of those types of books and found the vast majority to be theologically vacuous in problematic ways. Instead, Ashley adeptly navigates between these two dangerous alternatives. What he provides is a substantive, and profoundly readable, account of how postmodern philosophy can offer helpful resources for theological depth as a lived practice. Even though Ashley and I disagree about some theological specifics, his book invites charitable discourse and critical engagement in ways that are severely lacking in our current social situation. In that sense, it is a striking refusal to participate in the divisive, and deeply populist, culture wars of our contemporary world. Rather, in the spirit of the philosophers with whom he stands in conversation throughout the book, Ashley offers the reader to relate to Christianity as an existential invitation, a social challenge, and an existential task. In a time of megachurches, millionaire pastors, and rampant confusion about the boundary between evangelical religion and conservative politics, this book is a much-needed intervention.

Ashley takes critical aim at two temptations that he rightly sees as having infected Evangelicalism (especially as displayed in the Reformed tradition): egoistic individualism and intellectualized religious identity. His argument is that Christianity's focus on relationality and neighbor love is incompatible with a political individualism that primarily views others as either social obstacles or economic competitors. Similarly, following the existential philosophers upon whom he so deeply draws, Ashley rightly contends that faith is more a matter of lived investment than it is a matter of intellectual assent. Yes, it is important to hold truth beliefs (a virtue currently being actively undermined by political leaders widely supported by Evangelicals), but if we wanted just to believe true things, we could memorize the phone book. Christian truth is not ultimately a matter of abstract propositions but a matter of a lived example. When Jesus says, "I am the truth," as the philosopher Michel Henry so compellingly shows, Jesus positions Christianity as irreducible to signing faith statements in order to hold jobs at Christian colleges. Instead, Christian truth is a matter of the "costly grace" about which Bonhoeffer speaks.

Unfortunately, in a social context that operates according to an economic logic where everything is made meaningful only if it is profitable, where one's wealth determines one's moral status, and where power and influence are more a matter of marketing than substance, "costly grace" is a problem. Why pay more than you have to? Isn't the goal always to reduce cost and increase profits? Aren't large churches better than small ones? Surely pastors who have more followers on Instagram are more worthy of our attention, our time, and our devotion, right? It is this set of social values, priorities, and commitments that Ashley terms "Bourgeois Christianity." On this model, Christianity does not ask us to "take up our cross" but to download an app. Bourgeois Christians are not concerned with what Lee Camp terms "mere discipleship" because that requires cultivating humility, hospitality, and gratitude. Those values do not sell well. Instead, Bourgeois Christians either actively foster, or passively enable, a culture of fear, anger, and *ressentiment*. Bourgeois Christians are more worried about losing their social status, their political influence, and their epistemic certainty than they are about caring for the least of their neighbors. Indeed, the "least" are rarely able to contribute to the coffers in ways that facilitate hiring more pastors.

Bourgeois Christianity is *gross*.

First, it is a *gross* misunderstanding of the model of Jesus that positions power in powerlessness, rethinks the least as the greatest among us, and encourages love in the face of fear. Further, it is a *gross* misapplication of democratic politics such that it thinks democracy is more about enriching one's own "side" than it is about patiently hearing the challenge of moral and epistemic equals who see things differently. Finally, it is a *gross* misuse of philosophical and theological resources. It celebrates the establishment over the persecuted, the empowered over the marginal, and the whole over the broken. It wrongly thinks that a city on a hill is a nationalistic rallying cry, rather than a call to self-denial. It confuses the intellectual skill of using apologetic rhetorical tropes to expand one's tribe with the theological task of humbly navigating the human condition in the face of mysteries that will not be answered by theodicies.

Ashley strikingly highlights the characteristics of Bourgeois Christianity, offers a constructive diagnosis of the situation, and then critically reflects on philosophical and theological resources that might stand ready to help us move from the gross to the glorious. This book reminds us all what matters. It speaks to our deepest needs and reveals our deepest connections. It shows us why Derrida (and Kierkegaard, and Ricoeur, and Arendt, and many others) *should* be embraced in evangelical churches. They, along with Ashley himself, remind us that thinking well entails showing hospitality to the thought of others. They, along with Ashley himself, reveal what it means to love truth more than just being perceived as right. They, along with Ashley himself, require us to interrogate our conceptions of "God" that might get in the way of living faithfully.

Even though I approach this book as a professional philosopher, I learned a great deal from Ashley while reading it, and I would recommend it to almost anyone in my local church congregation. Combining such depth and accessibility is truly a remarkable feat. Ashley's authorial voice is witty without ever being sarcastic, humble while still displaying appropriate scholarly confidence, and invested in the tradition without simply being such an "insider" perspective that it loses critical awareness. In fact, perhaps that is the best way to frame things as you begin to read this book: It invites you to become aware. Become aware of what is going on, why it matters, and what you can do about it.

So, as the band Rage Against the Machine so eloquently puts it, "Wake up!"

And as we say in my Pentecostal churches, "Amen."

Acknowledgments

WRITING THIS BOOK AND preparing it for publication would not have been possible without the help of my friends. My colleague Charles Weigle read an early version of the book and offered helpful advice. Dr. Aaron Simmons of Furman University guided me through some postmodern philosophy issues. Dr. Richard Pratt of Third Millennium Ministries helped me understand some issues in contemporary Reformed thought. And Dr. Hunter Bailey offered encouraging words based on his review of the book. Dr. Diane Elliott helped me sharpen my prose, and Beverly Lillie organized the book to be ready for publication. I also thank Marc Jolley for recommending Wipf & Stock. I thank Wipf & Stock for the very professional way they go about publishing books. Most importantly, I thank my wife Ellen for all the hours she spent proofreading and correcting my work and all the years she was patient while I wrote this book.

Abbreviations

LCL   Loeb Classical Library

NICNT   New International Commentary on the New Testament

TDNT   *Theological Dictionary of the New Testament*. Edited by Gerhard Kittel and Gerhard Friedrich. Translated by Geoffrey W. Bromiley. 10 vols. Grand Rapids: Eerdmans, 1964–1976.

Introduction and Description of My Method

> We must not, then, as Christians, assume an attitude of antagonism toward the truths of reason, or the truths of philosophy, or the truths of science, or the truths of history, or the truths of criticism. As children of the light, we must be careful to keep ourselves open to every ray of light. If it is light, its source must be sought in him who is the true Light; if it is truth, it belongs of right to him who is the plenitude of truth.—B. B. Warfield[1]

THIS BOOK IS ABOUT unintended consequences and insidious effects. It is about those who send the wrong message when they think they are sending a biblical message and about doing the same thing over and over and expecting changed lives. It is about being entangled in your own tradition and stumbling over God's truth. It is about the snare of the familiar. This book exposes the deep undertow of paganism lurking beneath the evangelical knowledge culture that causes a neap tide of spirituality. This is paradoxical, and in this book, I describe how cultural paradoxes divert Evangelicals from serving God in the name of God. This book is about how paganism has seeped into Christian churches unnoticed. It is about worldliness.

Evangelicals have a problem. There is a serpent in the garden, and the serpent is worldliness, and the garden is the American church. Worldliness misleads Evangelicals in many ways, and in this book, I expose some of them. But I target the worldliness that is hard to understand, and it is hard to understand because it is paradoxical.

---

1. Warfield, *Selected Writings*, 2:463.

INTRODUCTION AND DESCRIPTION OF MY METHOD

A paradox is something that seems contradictory but turns out to be true. This book shows how the paradoxes of worldliness can twist Christian truth and the results churches get in teaching that truth. In this context something is paradoxical when you get the opposite result from what you expect. Or, put another way, what you believe is good and helpful and even sacred can promote worldliness and thwart spirituality. Sowing seeds to grow spiritual wheat instead yields worldly tares.

This kind of worldliness is not easy to understand. Many pastors don't understand it. More importantly, evangelical pastors and seminary professors can promote worldliness by the way they lead their churches and teach their students. Biblical preaching and church traditions can produce worldliness at spirituality's expense and defeat an embodied and existential[2] Christian life of loving neighbors.

Christianity is an embodied religion—remember the incarnate Christ. It calls Christians to use their bodies to love their neighbors. This demands action, and action requires more than having a correct biblical consciousness. Romans 12:1 explains embodied as presenting "your bodies a living and holy sacrifice, acceptable to God, which is your spiritual service of worship." An existential Christianity calls believers to devote their existence to their God. As St. Augustine says: "For whosoever has real existence, is this, is a keeper of God's commandments; and he who is not this, is nothing."[3] A disembodied faith unrooted in the believer's existence is the average Christianity that the world produces. But this worldliness hides in the shadows of paradoxes. For example, church traditions can promote a weak piety. This book shows the unintended consequences of well-intended actions.

The book also examines the unintended consequences of well-intended institutions like churches and seminaries and the American culture. Few, including myself, would argue against democracy and equality. But one of the unintended consequences of democracy as equality of conditions is a self-absorbed egotism and the failure of community that this self-centered individualism produces.

---

2. The word "existential" is used throughout this book. The meaning of the term is developed from the introduction to the last chapter. For now I will let the apostle Paul describe the existential Christian life: "Brethren, I do not regard myself as having laid hold of it yet; but one thing I do: forgetting what lies behind and reaching forward to what lies ahead, I press on toward the goal of the prize of the upward call of God in Christ Jesus" (Phil 3:13–14). See the last page of this introduction, 14n27, for another excellent definition of an existential Christianity.

3. Augustine, *City of God*, 713.

This individualism isolates speech from deed—talk but no walk. It isolates people from each other, especially those people the Bible calls neighbors. But there are no isolated individuals. Human life is public, shared, and possible only by a mutual language. Indeed, you cannot have biblical truth without language, and there is no language without people. Therefore, Christian experience cannot be private experience. The Christian life is not about focusing on one's mind at the expense of action.

To show the paradoxes of worldliness, I try to answer several questions. Why do churches that teach the gospel, preach verse-by-verse sermons, and exercise church discipline see changed minds but so few changed lives? Why do pastors in evangelical churches use biblical methods but still produce spiritual sluggards? And consistent with these questions, this book describes what it means to be a Christian and how hard it is to be faithful in America. Although how to become a Christian is common talk, what it means to be a Christian is not, in part because many Evangelicals believe that being a Christian is the same as becoming one, and that means "accepting Christ as your Savior." They are wrong.

One of the main reasons they are wrong is because they believe that being a Christian is a decision, when in fact it is a life, especially a life of serving God and neighbor in an ethical system called the kingdom of God. Being a Christian is fundamentally living for God and neighbor, empowered by God's enabling grace, seizing that grace, cultivating it, and expressing it in neighbor love. This glorifies God. This is the ethical imperative in God's kingdom of grace. Consequently, the kingdom of God is not a knowledge culture; it is a grace-empowered action culture. Sadly, it is often in churches where grace is most taught that it is least practiced.

In one important sense, this book responds to an insightful book written by Professor David Wells of Gordon-Conwell Seminary called *The Courage to Be Protestant*.[4] With alarm, Wells describes Evangelicalism in decline and tries to rally the faithful to rebuild the church with the charge to preach the word of God, administer the sacraments, and apply church discipline.[5] This will cure ailing churches.

The launch point for my argument, however, comes from a review of Wells's book by Professor Carl Trueman, formerly of Westminster Theological Seminary. In his review, Trueman replies to Wells's call to return to

---

4. This is an excellent book, but Wells is caught in the denominational thinking that blinds him to the limitations of his approach.

5. Wells, *Courage to Be Protestant*, 225.

a courageous Protestantism by saying that the world's carbon monoxide can co-opt even conservative, confessional types.[6] In other words, even in churches that teach the word, administer the sacraments, and discipline sinners, worldliness can find a comfortable home in believers' hearts. I explain why this is true, how it happens, and how ancient and modern pagan thought haunts the house of God and plagues his chosen people.

Some worldliness develops out of modern-age paganism. Modernity has attacked Christianity in many ways, and some of the gravest wounds are hidden. Evangelicals don't see them. But some modern philosophers have identified the problems and influences of modernity in ways that theologians usually miss. Protestants miss the deadfalls and eddies of paganism because they look in the wrong place. They float down the river of tradition, not realizing that the currents of ancient and modern paganism steer Christians into the wrong channel on the river of righteousness. Indeed, they are blind to the familiar.

As a result, some Protestant pastors and teachers too often have unwittingly embraced, rather than rejected, paganism's influence. In this book, philosophers and sociologists describe the mischief-making influences of the age that Evangelicals have missed.[7] Protestants often make good thinkers about theology but poor thinkers about culture; and paradoxically, you can fail when you do too much of what you do well. Indeed, theology, doctrine, and Bible knowledge can ensnare the feet of those called to enter by the narrow gate and walk the narrow way of the Christian life. In other words, theological depth can produce spiritual shallowness—another paradox of worldliness. This book tries to expose how contemporary evangelical thought and practices are swayed by pagan thought and practices. I go about the task in the following way.

First, I describe a type of worldliness that I call Bourgeois Christianity. Bourgeois Christianity includes a broad subset of American Evangelicalism beset by paganism. It takes believers out of the ethical kingdom of duty that Christ commands and slips them into the aesthetic realm of isolating knowledge and self-gratifying feelings. But understanding

---

6. Trueman, "Courageous Protestantism?"

7. My approach in using philosophical insights is consistent with the middle ground of an older Reformed view. Philosophy and theology are not parts of a whole, nor is philosophy necessarily contrary to theology. It can assist theological discussions. "Theology rules over philosophy, and this latter acts as a handmaid to and subserves the former" (Rehnman, "Alleged Rationalism," 260).

Bourgeois Christianity requires a complex diagnosis that takes many pages to explain and the reader's patience to understand.

To that end, I divide this book into two parts. Part 1 describes the paradoxes of evangelical and American cultures that produce Bourgeois Christianity and its mode of piety, which is an intellectualized and half-spirited way of serving God. Bourgeois Christianity is a dappled kind of Christianity, colored mostly by paganism with biblical highlights. Furthermore, bourgeois virtue characterizes Bourgeois Christianity. Bourgeois means middle class, and I argue in part 1 that evangelical virtue is mostly middle-class virtue. Self-control becomes the paramount virtue. Sin for Bourgeois Christians is what we ought not to have *done*. They neglect or disregard the sins of good acts left *undone*. Self-focus disrupts covenant focus, and the covenant is fundamental to the believer's relationship to God.

Evangelical virtue often is the old-style American individualism of working hard, being an upstanding citizen, having good morals and good manners, and attending church often. This fits well with the American civil religion, but loving one's neighbor is counter-cultural to the individualistic and self-absorbed narcissism of American culture. American individualism, both classical and therapeutic, blocks the way.

A religion of appearances replaces a religion of action, and words are taken for works. It is a convenient religion of taking, but not giving back, consuming, but not producing, and turning God into a means, not the End. Bourgeois Christians "believe" in the truth but rarely act on it, persevere in it, or sacrifice for it. But there is more in part 2.

Part 2 describes the Cartesian consciousness of Bourgeois Christianity. This is central to my argument and vital to understanding the emptiness of "biblically based" Bourgeois Christianity and its narrow knowledge culture. Part 2 describes the Christian knowledge culture found in a large subset of Evangelicals that reveals itself in an intellectualized Christianity. It is important to understand that this kind of intellectualism is completely consistent with the anti-intellectualism that has powerfully influenced much conservative Christian thinking for decades in American fundamentalists' circles. So I don't use the word "intellectualism" in the way that it is often understood. It expresses the idea that the way to serve God is with the mind, and having the proper biblical understanding or the right doctrine makes God happy with you. Emphasizing knowledge, correct biblical thinking, right doctrine, or what is often called in this book the biblically correct consciousness is worldly when thinking replaces doing.

Part 2 also explains how the modern view of the mind has replaced the biblical view of the heart as the pattern for piety. This pattern is pagan. Knowledge and virtue have become the same, or as a philosopher might describe it: the identity of knowledge and virtue. In other words, I am moral, righteous, or good because I believe the right ideas or have true knowledge. This idea has a long heritage in Western thought.[8] But making biblical knowledge the goal of piety has emerged among some Evangelicals as the way to serve God, to obey his commands, and to fulfill the covenant by having a correct biblical consciousness. We especially see this shallowness in some Reformed and dispensationalist churches, but it is common in many evangelical churches.

Hence, for Bourgeois Calvinists, Bourgeois dispensationalists, and others, the Christian life becomes a life of learning higher truth. Their main goal becomes thinking the correct thoughts. This is worldly. As one twentieth-century philosopher explains: "The modern era . . . made a terrible blunder by clinging to the belief that man's primary being consists in thinking, that his basic relationship with things is an intellectual relationship."[9] And as philosopher Ludwig Wittgenstein explains about our age, "Thinking is surrounded by a nimbus."[10] Thinking and thinkers enjoy a special aura. It is the new Gnosticism. The Christian life becomes a series of psychological events—feeling, learning, thinking, reflecting, and talking about what you know. The result: identifying Christian virtue with Christian knowledge and believing that godliness comes from having good theology and listening to sound preaching. Unfortunately, this thinking focus does not necessarily promote spiritual maturity; it too often ends in an enlightened impotency.

Moreover, this modern way of serving God and working in his kingdom is a new way of understanding the covenantal duties of God's people. It becomes a thinking down the narrow way and not a walking down it (Matt 7:13–14). But at the same time, it is an old view because the idea that thinking is the highest doing is a Greek idea.[11] In too many evangelical churches, Plato is still behind the scenes pulling the strings of thought. And a denomination's tradition can clot biblical truth and block it from the heart, producing a doctrinally enlightened mind that blocks love

---

8. Berlin, *Roots of Romanticism*, 137–38.
9. Ortega, *Man and Crisis*, 160.
10. Wittgenstein, *Philosophical Investigations*, 49. A nimbus is a halo.
11. Heidegger, *Question Concerning Technology*, 164.

flowing from a gracious heart. Learning biblical truth is very important, but privileging the mind and neglecting action are unchristian. Indeed, among Bourgeois Christians, focusing on learning more about the Bible and denominational distinctives can replace loving more, and a kind of forgetting others comes with this learning. It avoids the serious thinking needed to build a covenant-embracing Christian life.

The neighbor is forgotten because "neighbor" becomes a biblical concept to learn, rather than a person to love. Despite all their knowledge, Bourgeois Christians have little existential understanding of the truth that "the whole Law is fulfilled in one word, 'You shall love your neighbor as yourself'" (Gal 5:14). And this follows from the spirit of the age explained in my chapters on democracy as equality of conditions, the therapeutic culture, the thin theology of American revivalism, and especially the Cartesian mind/body dualism. This book describes one of our culture's dominant effects: the personal disengagement from our neighbors because people are so focused on themselves.

This problem flows in part from the fact that Western philosophy has created a shallow understanding of what truth is. Evangelicals do not understand that truth is *aletheia* or unconcealedness. Hence, they misuse biblical words and phrases without understanding them existentially because they never incarnate the words in their lives. The conceptual truth of doctrine and theology becomes the real truth—the truth of words, rather than the truth of lives engaged in relationships. And as part 2 shows, the more conceptual Christianity becomes, in other words, the more doctrinal and theological it becomes, the further it turns from an existential faith, because an overintellectualized faith breeds shallow believers. It hides the existential truths of Christian living.[12] Some call these shallow believers the "frozen chosen." This is an oxymoron that arises from the paradox. The chosen, who are called to everyday action, can't be frozen. Overemphasizing knowledge, however, has a chilling effect.

Consequently, I reject the knowledge-culture premise that more Bible knowledge means more spiritual growth; or that the more Bible you know, the better Christian you are; or that the best thing you can do during the week is go to a Bible study. (I don't reject, however, the importance of learning or Bible study. Bible ignorance is not bliss.) The knowledge culture

---

12. Professor Stanley Rosen concludes: "The closer I come to formal structures, and the more I talk about them, the more I conceal them—that is, the more I replace the web of forms or Ideas by the web of concepts or linguistic constructions" (*Hermeneutics as Politics*, 55).

emphasizes the pagan idea of the identity of knowledge and virtue, and it results in a beating-the-air kind of boxing (1 Cor 9:26). Indeed, knowledge often leads to the hollowness of Phariseeism. The priest and the Levite, both trained in the law, ignored the wounded man on the road, while the despised Samaritan bound his wounds, carried him to a haven, and paid for his care (Luke 10:30–37).[13] The priest and the Levite had the knowledge but not the will. They lacked an ethics of action, which is no ethics at all, because as Augustine says, "The right will is, therefore, well-directed love, and the wrong will is ill-directed love."[14]

Understanding biblical truth in an existential way is a kind of willing that expresses God's love and the truth of Christian ethics. It is existential because it is fundamental to a believer's existence. It engages the will in action.

The word "ethics" may sound odd to some ears because Christian ethics implies duty, and duty seems to contradict grace. But as Professor R. C. Sproul explains, "Christianity is concerned with morality, righteousness, and ethics."[15] And these are existential concerns that require action, not just a correct consciousness or a biblically furnished mind.

Indeed, the mind focus degrades Scripture's ethical emphasis, the action emphasis, and warps the expressive nature of Christian living. Bourgeois Christians bring this worldly intellectualism to many churches every Sunday, and it often gets reaffirmed by a hidden or covert message that implies what Christians know is what counts. They don't understand the power of our self-absorbed culture or the Cartesian dualism that separates the mind from the body and things, and that consequently separates the Bourgeois Christians from their neighbors. They don't understand the pagan culture's power over them.

As Christian philosopher and theologian David Bentley Hart observes:

> We all inhabit cultural and linguistic worlds that determine to a great extent what we think important, how we see reality, what fundamental premises we assume, and even what we most deeply desire. We are not entirely confined to these worlds—we are living

---

13. The priest and the Levite knew their Old Testament duty to love neighbors and to help widows, orphans, and aliens.

14. Augustine, *City of God*, 449.

15. Sproul, "3 Types of Legalism," para. 11.

souls, not merely machines—but it requires considerable effort to see beyond their horizons.[16]

Hart explains the power that society has over individuals, and believing in God and the Bible does not exempt someone from this control. Too many Evangelicals can't see the narrow horizon of culture and its subverting power because they see no reason to do so. If they reject abortion, gay marriage, and the Democratic Party, and have said the Sinner's Prayer, they are fine with God. But they confuse political beliefs with biblical truth and create a cultural Christianity.

Furthermore, it should not surprise Evangelicals that they can't see the culture's power surrounding them. As Presbyterian professor Bill Fullilove explains, Christians are barely conscious of the culture, much less know how to deal with it biblically.[17] So they sit in the pews and have no idea about how a cultural Christianity directs their thinking but not their doing, which is their spiritual undoing. And because of culture's subverting power, many biblical words and phrases have lost their punch—another paradox.

Common biblical words and phrases like "being saved," "believe in Jesus," "growing in grace," "accepting Christ," and "saving faith" have lost their force in the crowded traffic on the expressways of pagan culture.[18] The culture has rendered these phrases stale, and this staleness leads to a spiritual dryness. These words carry little salt and dim light.

But I didn't discover this word problem. Calvinist John J. Murray noted over forty-five years ago: "Never in the history of the church has so much been said to so many with so little effect! . . . We are using language that to us, and for the present at least, has lost its real meaning."[19] Also, twentieth-century philosopher Martin Heidegger says that the language used to talk about being is in general "worn out and used up."[20] Danish philosopher and theologian Søren Kierkegaard observed the same problem in Lutheran churches in Denmark one hundred years before Heidegger. Kierkegaard describes it this way: "Just as an old man who has lost his teeth

---

16. Hart, *Atheist Delusions*, 19.

17. Presentation at "Equip Conference," First Presbyterian Church, Macon, Oct. 24–26, 2014.

18. As Calvinist Robert More Jr. explains: "In one of the greatest verbal confusions in the history of the Christian Church saving faith had thus become equated with obeying 'the altar call'!" ("Altar Call," 33).

19. Murray, "We Pray," 1.

20. Heidegger, "Fundamental Question of Metaphysics," 3:250.

now munches with the help of the stumps, so the modern Christian language about Christianity has lost the power of the energetic terminology to bite—and the whole thing is toothless 'maundering.'"[21]

In other words, Bourgeois Christians do not understand the familiar—those biblical words that they use without thinking about what they mean. The biblespeak culture cues Evangelicals about what to say and when to say it, so they sound spiritual. They do not understand that these words carry more than knowledge; they impose ethics, and ethics commands action, and action is a duty. Love is not a concept, a doctrine, an opinion, or a state of mind. Love is action.

Applied to the contemporary church, these weak words are shibboleths, or Christian passwords that Evangelicals speak to prove their spirituality, or words some pastors use that, paradoxically, can confuse their members. These shibboleths promote the thin theology of American revivalism. But they are not just ways of talking; they are ways of thinking that lead to an average kind of Christianity, and this average kind of Christianity is the hidden enemy of biblical Christianity.

Consequently, too often pastors sound forth clichés from their pulpits, but their words float off like echoes. The meanings of the words they preach get scrambled by the cultural clatter of the pagan age. And even as Professor Wells admits: "I have underestimated how remote a robust, biblical faith of a Protestant kind has actually become to many people today."[22]

This atrophy of God's word is one of the reasons for this anemic Protestantism, and that Wells has underestimated the problem shows its hidden nature and how even well-trained Christians do not understand the crisis. And because biblical words often are trite, I attack this problem by using words not commonly found in evangelical talk, like "existential," "embodied," "expressive," "embedded," and "incarnated," or phrases like "seeing-as-understanding" and "hearing-then-doing." (All these terms will be described later.) So I'm pushing back the bulwarks of the evangelical religion of the mind to describe the body's centrality in serving God.

Another important characteristic of my approach is that rather than relying on some theologians who can create and perpetuate the problems, I recruit philosophers and sociologists, some Christian and some not, to explain the modern-age contagion that afflicts the church.[23] (My book

---

21. Kierkegaard, *Concluding Unscientific Postscript*, 1:363.
22. Wells, *Courage to Be Protestant*, 217.
23. This is not a novel approach. Even a brief look at the index in Calvin's *Institutes*

also has hundreds of biblical references and images.) Even if these thinkers do not use the word "sin" or believe in the fall, they describe both well. They understand the modern age better than many evangelical theologians because these philosophers focus on questions about existence and being and consciousness and relationships and how modernity provokes emptiness in the culture.

What I am describing reveals the unintended consequences of the sincere efforts of godly people who do not understand the age or how strongly paganism pumps through the bloodstream of evangelical culture. Paganism creates an intellectualized Christianity that concentrates on the believer's mind while the spirit languishes. It is an ever-learning but never-coming to the knowledge of the truth worked out in an embodied Christian life. For too many Evangelicals, it is paganism's progress, not pilgrims' progress.

To combat this, part 2 describes the problem of focusing on the believer's consciousness and the intellectualized inaction this creates at the expense of relationships of love. I will show what is hidden, what is concealed in the way truth is revealed in even the most orthodox churches.

As noted above, this is a book about the unintended consequences of well-intended people. But it is also about the duty of those people to become aware of and deal with those unintended consequences. Time is running out. Indeed, paganism's star is in the ascendant in America, guiding the culture, and Evangelicalism is waning into a flickering faith and wavering hope that darkens into a twilight piety.

More than fifty years ago, Professor Paul Helm, another Calvinist, wrote:

> Contemporary problems and challenges press upon us, and to hide from them would be foolish; but to hide from them in the name of Christian truth is much worse. Do we seriously think that we can act responsibly in 1968 simply by taking down the appropriate book from our shelves? . . . If, for whatever reason, we remain transfixed by the seventeenth-century situation then our Reformed and evangelical witness will take on the form of an elaborate parlour game, a sort of religious "Scrabble." Whatever we might think about our life and witness we shall in effect have become a middle-class Protestant cult catering for an eccentric minority. We will be engulfed and forgotten, and will deserve to be.[24]

---

shows that Calvin cited many pagan philosophers and writers, like Plato and Cicero.

24. Helm, "On Being a Contemporary Christian," 17–18.

Helm spoke this prophetic word for naught because the parlor game continues apace in many evangelical churches distracted by doctrinal scrabbling and comfort catering as the raging seas of culture swamp Evangelicals. This kind of skinny intellectualism thins the thickness of covenantal duty. Sadly, the churches that think they are the most orthodox and have the brightest theological lights often wander in a desert of spiritual darkness and stumble into the tar pits of the age. And as Helm says, some intellectualist churches rely on nostalgia for the old way—a naïve yearning for some glorious past. But as one German philosopher explains: "Fidelity to the old is not proved by repeating it but by giving it new expression in word and deed at each historical juncture."[25] A new expression requires action. But before completing this section on my method, several important points remain.

First, no one should conclude that I deny that salvation comes by grace alone through faith in Christ alone or that I argue that works save. Books about God's grace abound, and I see no reason to write another one. On the other hand, this book highlights what many Evangelicals don't understand: "Even so faith, if it has no works, is dead, being by itself" (Jas 2:17). Unfortunately, they don't realize that this is also grace. Too many Evangelicals deny "that faith without works is useless" (Jas 2:20) because they accept the thin theology of American revivalism—say a prayer and you are saved. But the opposite of a Christian knowledge culture is not a Christian ignorance culture; it is an embodied and expressive action culture of love at work in faith through grace. Moreover, the opposite of truth is not only ignorance; it is also unrighteousness. And righteousness involves action, not a state of mind. And very importantly: this book is about grace but not in the way many Evangelicals understand it. It is not about God's grace for me; it is about believers' grace for neighbors.

Second, although this book describes American culture, it is not for the culture. Rather, it is for the evangelical camp. It is intramural. In my view, outside the camp, pluralism should prevail because pluralism is a form of grace and agape love, God's love.

Third, I use "love your neighbor" throughout this book because it is the royal law (Jas 2:8) demanded by the Great Commandment (Matt 22:36–40) and because loving one's neighbor is loving God (Matt 25:40). This godly love for neighbor and God forms a golden alloy. Moreover, God makes the neighbor relationship transcendent. It is transcendent because God's love joins and empowers our love to our neighbors. But more important for

---

25. Horkheimer, *Critique of Instrumental Reason*, 155–56.

understanding this book, "loving your neighbor" stands for that constellation of Christian duties summarized in the stars of the covenant, the kingdom of God, service to God, and sacrifice for God. It is the touchstone of Christian duty to people and to God. It is action flowing from a loving heart filled with gratitude to God. The Samaritan figured it out; why can't so many Evangelicals (Luke 10:33–37)? This book answers that question.

Fourth, many Evangelicals claim that the Bible is the infallible and inerrant word of God and essential to the faith. For Calvinists it provides the basis for faith and practice. Throughout this book, the words of Scripture serve as a mirror to see how well Bourgeois Christians live the Christian life according to their own book.

Fifth, my readers must beware the genetic fallacy. A person commits this fallacy when he or she rejects an idea because of whose idea it is, not because it is wrong. This is a fallacy, or bad thinking, because of what Calvinists call common grace. Even pagans can know truth. Moreover, this fallacy is part of the scandal and shallowness of the evangelical mind and what B. B. Warfield warns against in the quote at the beginning of this introduction.

Sixth, everything that follows describes our age and how it directs our attention to ourselves and diverts Christians from loving neighbors. Neighbor love is the essence of God's law; neighbor neglect is the quintessence of worldliness, and I will show how American culture drives neglect. Indeed, pagan culture has colonized the evangelical church, and many of the natives have surrendered. This surrender to the world is not new; read Judges, Isaiah, Jeremiah, and Ezekiel.

A creaking conformism and lazy emptiness are stealing down the aisles of many evangelical churches. They are shelters for a decaying Christianity. In these churches you find what Samuel Taylor Coleridge describes as "manifold motions making little speed."[26] Evangelicals need a revival of the love-giving life that Christ lived and proclaimed. They need to stop sounding good and start doing good. They need to enter the vital relationship that he offers through the Spirit. Unfortunately, many Evangelicals have caught hold of the spirit of modernity. That spirit leads to an ever-diminishing role of personal duty and responsibility.

Finally, Søren Kierkegaard explains the point of my book very well:

> On the other hand, what I am speaking about is very plain and simple, namely, that truth is for the particular individual only as

---

26. "Psyche," in Coleridge, *Poems and Prose*, 205.

he himself produces it in action. If the truth is for the individual in any other way, or if he prevents the truth from being for him in that way, we have a phenomenon of the demonic. Truth has always had many loud proclaimers, but the question is whether a person will in the deepest sense acknowledge the truth, will allow it to permeate his whole being, will accept all its consequences, and not have an emergency hiding place for himself and a Judas kiss for the consequence.[27]

To that end, this book is an uplifting and upbuilding discourse. "Build up, build up, prepare the way," says God. But to prepare the way, God also says, "Remove every obstacle out of the way of my people" (Isa 57:14). Worldliness obstructs his children's way. To remove it requires some cautery, some burning and cutting, that leads to healing and restoring and the abundant life that Jesus offers in vital union with him. This book shows the power, the beauty, and the opportunities in God's kingdom that many Evangelicals miss.

---

27. Kierkegaard, *Concept of Anxiety*, 138. This is an excellent description of an existential Christianity.

Part I: **How American Culture Infects Evangelicals**

Chapter 1 Democratic Culture: Democracy as Equality of Conditions

THIS CHAPTER DESCRIBES SOME secular characteristics of our democratic culture that influence Evangelicals. But even though I use the word "democracy," this chapter has nothing to do with candidates, elections, or governments; rather it explains the power that democracy as *equality of conditions* wields over the lives of Americans—their being, their consciousness, their everyday living. The democracy of equality of conditions is an unhealthy form of the fundamental principle of equality. Hence, this chapter is not a critique of equality but rather of a malign form of equality that afflicts the evangelical church.

Alexis de Tocqueville's *Democracy in America* describes democracy as equality of conditions. It is a prophetic book written about America in the 1830s when Tocqueville traveled the country to see democracy at work. Following Tocqueville's analysis, this chapter outlines five characteristics of American individualism and the problems these characteristics cause for Evangelicals. Tocqueville shows how equality of conditions structures culture and directs the clamoring and yearnings of most Americans. As he explains in his introduction, nothing "struck me more forcefully than the equality of conditions." He saw it "as the original fact from which each particular fact seemed to derive."[1] Indeed, the second half of his

---

1. Tocqueville, *Democracy in America*, 3. Tocqueville and *Democracy in America* are both still widely esteemed in conservative academic circles.

eight-hundred-page book describes the control that equality of conditions imposes on "inclinations and ideas."[2]

But more important than Tocqueville's historical analysis, equality of conditions still exerts its power by launching Americans on a vector towards an island of self-absorbed individualism, the therapist's couch, or both. These books describe the results: *The Lonely Crowd, Alone Together, Bowling Alone, The Pursuit of Loneliness, Therapy Culture, The Closing of the American Mind, The Narcissism Epidemic, Generation Me,* and *In Therapy We Trust: America's Obsession with Self-Fulfillment*. The titles reflect the poverty of American culture and the forces that inflict decline. The authors expose the depth of the American malaise. In a way, they follow Tocqueville's steps by observing, analyzing, and critiquing contemporary American society.[3]

Even though much of what Tocqueville wrote about America in the 1830s doesn't apply today, his ideas about the power of equality of conditions and how this equality structures the goals and lifestyles of Americans remain true. Too often the individualism of equality steers Americans along a cultural turnpike toward Vanity Fair's pleasures and the stalled-out self.[4] The desire for equality can drive people into lifestyles and promote opinions and passions as it did in Tocqueville's day.

Tocqueville describes five characteristics of people living under equality of conditions. His key passage distinguishing egoism from individualism is well known and merits quoting:

> Individualism is a reflective and tranquil sentiment that disposes each citizen to cut himself off from the mass of his fellow men and withdraw into the circle of family and friends, so that, having created a little society for his own use, he gladly leaves the larger society to take care of itself.
>
> Egoism is born of blind instinct; individualism proceeds from erroneous judgment rather than depraved sentiment. Its source lies as much in defects of the mind as in vices of the heart.

---

2. Tocqueville, *Democracy in America*, 479.

3. Tocqueville did not condemn everything that he saw about American culture. In fact, he found many encouraging qualities, but many of those have disappeared, especially in the past fifty years.

4. This chapter is not a critique of democracy or of equality. This chapter critiques democracy as equality of conditions because of the type of individualism it produces.

DEMOCRATIC CULTURE: DEMOCRACY AS EQUALITY OF CONDITIONS

> Egoism shrivels the seed of all the virtues; individualism at first dries up only the source of the public virtues, but in the long run it attacks and destroys all the others and in the end will be subsumed in egoism.
>
> Egoism is a vice as old as the world. It is not to any great extent more characteristic of one form of society than of another.
>
> Individualism is democratic in origin, and it threatens to develop as conditions equalize. . . . Again and again it leads him [the citizen] back to himself and threatens ultimately to imprison him altogether in the loneliness of his own heart.[5]

Tocqueville explains the causes of empty individualism and its consequences. Admittedly, many find no problem with what he describes. But it is a problem for Evangelicals, whom God commands to embrace neighbors rather than to retreat into a cloistered individualism. And as I will show, many Evangelicals live in a new monasticism of the mind encircled by walls of self-interest.

According to Tocqueville, this kind of one-dimensional or closed-society individualism originates in the mind from a defective understanding that tends to reflect but not act. Most importantly, it cuts one off from the mass of other people and causes individuals to withdraw into a narrow circle of friends and family to create their own little societies. It uproots and disconnects people. This equality-driven individualism disrupts the duty to love the neighbor. But this withdrawing into a tight circle of family and friends has a biblical parallel that Jesus condemns and Bourgeois Christians practice. It is called gentile love.

In the Sermon on the Mount, Jesus teaches: "For if you love those who love you, what reward do you have? Do not even the tax collectors do the same? If you greet only your brothers, what more are you doing than others? Do not even the Gentiles do the same?" (Matt 5:46–47). Loving those who love you, caring about those close to you, and helping those who help you follow the inverted, closed-society individualism that equality of conditions generates. Gentile love is self-oriented and characterized by failing to love neighbors. (Of course, loving your family and friends is very good, unless your love stops there.)

Consequently, dwelling on the self results in denying Christ's command to "not merely look out for your own personal interests, but also for the interests of others" (Phil 2:4). As Tocqueville explains, this kind of

---

5. Tocqueville, *Democracy in America*, 585–87.

equality "tends to isolate people from one another, so that each individual is inclined to think only of himself."[6] Here is how Tocqueville describes it: "For him, his children and personal friends comprise the entire human race. As for the remainder of his fellow citizens, he lives alongside them but does not see them. He touches them but does not feel them. He exists only in himself and for himself, and if he still has a family, he no longer has a country."[7] This describes what Charles Taylor calls the closed-in or buffered self.[8]

Is it like this today in America? Writing in 2004, sociologist Frank Furedi describes our culture in this way: "The most significant feature of therapeutic culture is not so much the promotion [of self] but the distancing of the self from others. In this it consistently crystallizes the contemporary mood of individuation. Therapeutic culture both reflects and promotes the trend towards fragmentation and alienation."[9] Explaining further, he says: "In its therapeutic form, individualism encourages the distancing of self from friends, family members and other potential intimates."[10] Indeed, it has gotten worse. Tocqueville saw Americans withdrawing into little societies of families and friends, but even families don't hold people together today. About 50 percent of marriages in America end in divorce, and divorce fragments the family, the basic unit of society.

A fragmented culture is an atomistic culture, and although Furedi describes a therapeutic culture, democracy as equality of conditions has, in part, created this therapeutic culture and fragmented our society. Additionally, a culture deeply soaked in the rum of the therapeutic is one part of the narcissistic endgame of equality of conditions and the rampant focus on well-being that cuts many off from caring for others.

Following hard on a self-focusing individualism and adding to it, Tocqueville observes that equality of conditions inspires the American goal of devoting the self to personal well-being, which signals a return to ancient pagan Eudemonism or an emphasis on human flourishing. He describes Americans' heat for personal well-being: "Of all the passions that equality brings into being or encourages, there is . . . one that it causes everyone to feel with particular ardor, namely, the passion for well-being. The passion for well-being is a striking and indelible feature of every democratic

---

6. Tocqueville, *Democracy in America*, 503.
7. Tocqueville, *Democracy in America*, 818.
8. See ch. 6 for a discussion of the buffered self.
9. Furedi, *Therapy Culture*, 21.
10. Furedi, *Therapy Culture*, 171.

age."[11] Americans' "minds are universally preoccupied with meeting the body's every need and attending to life's little comforts."[12] In fact, "love of well-being has become the national and dominant taste. The mainstream of the human passions runs in this direction and sweeps everything along with it."[13] These passions still describe many Americans today. And Eva S. Moskowitz exposes this national mission in her book, *In Therapy We Trust: America's Obsession with Self-Fulfillment*. You need only look at a magazine rack to see the passion for self-fulfillment.

Think about the messages in these popular magazines: *Well Being Journal, Better Homes and Gardens, Good Housekeeping, Self, Cosmopolitan, In Style, Glamour, Vogue, Allure, Teen Vogue, Essence, Elle, Vanity Fair, Health, Women's Health, Men's Health, Men's Fitness, Fitness RX for Men, GQ, Esquire, Maxim, Playboy, Food and Wine, Nylon, Harper's Bazaar, Town and Country*, and *O, The Oprah Magazine*. They commonly expose and foment the whims and fashions of the moment for readers trying to find hope in the Age of Nothingness. For example, the May 2017 edition of *Health* offers these articles to improve their readers' well-being: "Best Abs Ever," "3 Easy Ways to Walk Off Weight," "Get Your Body Back!," "#1 Trick for Deeper Sleep," "Self-Care Tips That Reboot You," and "Flattering Swimsuits for All!" And as sociologist Eva Illouz explains, in a therapeutic culture, self-development is a right.[14]

But the Christian neighbor duty thwarts this national pursuit, and as Tocqueville says, individualism can block the soul from God.[15] How does equality of conditions cause the self-focus of the Me mentality? The social and economic mobility of democracies creates the drive for well-being and self-fulfillment.

According to Tocqueville, the social mobility that began with the rise of democracy produces this stunting individualism because it incites and enables certain lifestyles and goals. And although people believe that they act freely, the thrall of culture drives many along the relentless track of restless lives. It breeds a passion for getting ahead, a striving for easy gratification, and neighbor envy—and envying your neighbor hinders loving your neighbor.

11. Tocqueville, *Democracy in America*, 507.
12. Tocqueville, *Democracy in America*, 617.
13. Tocqueville, *Democracy in America*, 619.
14. Illouz, *Cold Intimacies*, 45.
15. Tocqueville, *Democracy in America*, 621.

Furthermore, Tocqueville describes the passion and striving for material goods that animates Americans:

> [The American] clings to the goods of this world as though assured of not dying, yet he is in such haste to grasp the ones that come his way that he seems almost to suffer from perpetual fear of passing away before finding time to enjoy them. He grasps at everything but embraces nothing and soon lets things slip from his grasp so that he may go chasing after new pleasures.[16]

Americans seek quick success and have difficulty overcoming the urges of the moment.[17] "The taste for material gratifications . . . [is] the primary source of that secret restlessness revealed by the actions of Americans and the inconstancy they exhibit every day."[18]

Think how busy most Americans are. Think how busy they keep their children, and Kierkegaard says busyness is worldliness.[19] Worldliness is servitude, cultural captivity for many Evangelicals. They are caught up in the moment and don't strive for the eternal.[20]

But the problem involves more than busyness. Because of the drive for success, the quest for this world's goods, and striving to get ahead of the neighbor, democracy arouses envy. Envy arises because equality of conditions promotes a restless ambition to get ahead in a highly mobile society.[21] Understanding a society that is mobile and not hierarchical is important for understanding Tocqueville's view of individualism's roots.

Social mobility is central to Tocqueville's analysis about how equality of conditions creates a restless and selfish society. For him a mobile society does not involve people moving from place to place. Rather it is a society in which people can move up and down socially and economically compared to their peers. This mobility enables people to change station, rank, power, and wealth. To explain this mobility, he distinguishes American democratic society from French aristocratic society before the French Revolution.

In the old French aristocratic society, everyone was linked together in layers of dependence among the classes. There was no individualism in aristocracies because everyone belonged in a group or class and did not

---

16. Tocqueville, *Democracy in America*, 625.
17. Tocqueville, *Democracy in America*, 498.
18. Tocqueville, *Democracy in America*, 626.
19. Kierkegaard, *Works of Love*, 105.
20. Kierkegaard, *Upbuilding Discourses*, 92.
21. Tocqueville, *Democracy in America*, 520–21.

understand themselves as isolated persons.[22] French aristocratic society was hierarchical and characterized by personal bonds; democratic society is in flux with limited bonds. The aristocratic hierarchy imposed relationships, stations, and duties on everyone. The king had a duty to the nobility and the nobility to the king. The nobility had a duty to their peasants, and peasants served the aristocrats. The aristocrat was born into his station in society, as were kings and peasants. And because of that society's immobility, almost everyone stayed in the position into which they were born with little opportunity to move up.

Prerevolutionary France was an immobile society with cultural walls built against social change. The peasant, his son, and grandson will always be peasants with little chance to progress up the social or economic ladder. And, most important for Tocqueville's analysis, because they have no chance to advance in life, they have no ambition to try. This leads poor people to focus on religion or life in another world. With few economic prospects, they don't strive for personal well-being.[23]

But when democracy replaces kings and aristocrats, it also ends the social hierarchy and its mutual duties and benefits. Life opens to new social and financial possibilities for everyone. The rich can lose their wealth, and the poor can gain wealth. This sparks the pursuit for well-being, especially for the middle class.[24] The middle class can now attain privileges once held only by nobility, and they stampede to get more, or what used to be called "keeping up with the Joneses." It is the American dream: dreaming about me and mine and my aesthetic pursuits, my success, my money, and the toys it can buy.

So in democracies many people try to escape their original condition, and ambition becomes universal.[25] Paradoxically, the freedom of individualism often leads to a servitude to things, and with all their striving to become authentic, they end up synthetic, plastic selves, molded by advertising and the consumer economy. Indeed, people become commodities. And as I will show later, this creates a society of lonely hearts, which means many lonely neighbors who need love. But it gets worse.

Loving one's neighbor is a central tenet of Christianity. Self-centered, gratification-oriented individuals see neighbor love as an obstacle to

22. Tocqueville, *Old Regime*, 96.
23. Tocqueville, *Democracy in America*, 618.
24. Tocqueville, *Democracy in America*, 618.
25. Tocqueville, *Democracy in America*, 738.

success. The neighbor duty gets in the way of ambition, and neighbors take time. Time is a commodity for the middle class, and like money, one must use it carefully. Indeed, as Tocqueville explains, one who has given his heart "to the quest for the goods of this world is always in a hurry, for he has but a limited time to find, possess, and enjoy them."[26] Tocqueville shows how equality of conditions and individualism trigger a worldly Christianity and how they can undermine piety. But Tocqueville describes another problem—a problem with thinking.

Many Americans don't know how to think critically. Tocqueville describes thinking or, more specifically, the lack of thinking, and says that democracy impels people both to new ways of thinking and to not thinking at all. When they do think, they generally operate based on a few general ideas or great causes followed by any number of general notions. This is especially true about religious beliefs.[27] (I will show how general ideas about salvation fail in ch. 4, "Evangelical Populism and the Thin Theology of American Revivalism.")

Busyness is a key reason for Americans' failure to think. "Men who live in ages of equality have much curiosity and little leisure. Their lives are so practical, so complicated, so agitated, and so active that little time remains for them to think. Men in democratic centuries love general ideas because they eliminate the need to study particular cases."[28] Biblical general ideas become abstractions and shibboleths or passwords that prevail in a Bourgeois Christian culture. You learn the concept, you get the idea, and you are done. Common biblical terms and phrases are so familiar that they become passwords, and their meaning is lost.

Philosopher G. W. F. Hegel describes the problem with the familiar in this way: "The familiar, just because it is familiar, is not cognitively understood. The commonest way in which we deceive either ourselves or others about understanding is by assuming something as familiar, and accepting it on that account; . . . such knowing never gets anywhere, and it knows not why." As Hegel further explains, this kind of thinking is "moving only on their surface."[29] Hegel understands that the familiar hides the

---

26. Tocqueville, *Democracy in America*, 626. He goes on to say: "Private life in democratic times is so active, so agitated, so filled with desires and labors that individuals have virtually no energy or leisure left for political life" (*Democracy in America*, 793). The same applies to kingdom work.

27. Tocqueville, *Democracy in America*, 492.

28. Tocqueville, *Democracy in America*, 498.

29. Hegel, *Phenomenology of Spirit*, 18.

truth, and he says specifically that the familiar hides the truth about God. This is another paradox.

Finally, about this thinking deficit, Tocqueville says: "Habitual inattention must be regarded as the greatest defect of the democratic mind."[30] This thinking failure is epidemic among Evangelicals.[31] Consequently, it is rare to find a good Berean in evangelical churches. Luke identified the Bereans as the noble-minded ones who eagerly received the word and who examined the Scriptures daily to see if the teaching was true (Acts 17:11). Armed now with Tocqueville's analysis, consider some special problems that confront churches in America.

First, Christian duty contradicts individualism's me focus, so Bourgeois Christians must reconcile contrary claims on their time. As Tocqueville explains, the weakness of the human mind wants to "buy peace at the expense of logic . . . [so as men submit] certain of their religious beliefs to some authority, [they] will seek to exempt other beliefs from that same authority, and [they] will allow their minds to fluctuate erratically between obedience and liberty."[32] The Evangelical must ask, "How Christian am I willing to be?" Or, "How much of my time and pleasure am I willing to give up to serve God?" Which controls, God's commands or my desires? But Christian identity is not individuality. It is instead an identity within a unity, and the unity is a community of neighbors, both the saved and the lost.

Second, and Tocqueville's most important point on this issue, the individualistic society limits how much the church can criticize the getting-and-spending, me-focused spirit of individualism. As equality increases, "it becomes increasingly important for religion not only to remain studiously aloof from the daily course of business but also to avoid unnecessary conflict with generally accepted ideas and with the enduring interests of the masses, because common opinion seems increasingly to be the foremost of powers, and the most irresistible."[33] In other words, criticizing the American way endangers the church and limits how aggressive preachers can be in attacking the spirit of individualism and the sacred goal of well-being. This passion is

---

30. Tocqueville, *Democracy in America*, 718.

31. Interestingly, Martin Heidegger explains why people no longer seek God: "They can no longer seek because they no longer think" (*Question Concerning Technology*, 112). This is consistent with Mark Noll's analysis in *The Scandal of the Evangelical Mind* and the lack of evangelical thinking. It is part of the age.

32. Tocqueville, *Democracy in America*, 510–11.

33. Tocqueville, *Democracy in America*, 508.

so strong that if religious leaders try to hinder their members from pursuing the world's goods, they will destroy the church.[34]

Many pastors understand this threat but never acknowledge it. They realize the culture limits what they preach and how Christian they can ask their congregation to be. But they can dodge this threat by preaching exegetical sermons week by week for years without ever having to contradict the individualistic spirit of the age. Consequently, many evangelical preachers proclaim Scripture every Sunday without challenging their congregations. They preach, but they don't meddle. This is part of the problem of taking biblical truth out of the cultural context and out of the ethical sphere—the action sphere—and moving it into the aesthetic sphere that requires only appreciating the beauty of the word or a good sermon, not obeying it.

For example, a recent graduate of a conservative Presbyterian seminary enjoys teaching about how Jesus is hidden in the Old Testament, something he learned from a seminary professor. But he fails to realize that emphasizing the beauty of Christ in the Old Testament can fall into the aesthetic trap that hides the demanding Old Testament ethical teaching. Thus, preaching becomes paradoxical: members hear the truth every Sunday, but they don't hear the truth they need most to battle the culture. And even more, most of them hear it only aesthetically, not ethically.

Too many pastors fear controversy or "opening a can of worms," as one Baptist preacher described it to me. Many preachers know what sells and what doesn't in our twenty-first-century consumer society, and as Tocqueville says, "I reproach equality not for leading men into the pursuit of forbidden pleasures but for absorbing them entirely in the search for permitted ones."[35] And further, "People want to be as well off as possible in this world without renouncing their chances in the next."[36] This is Bourgeois Christianity, and Bourgeois Christians live in the musty cellar of self.

An individualistic society also encourages this-worldly desires and discourages covenantal action. As Tocqueville notes, "Passions, needs, upbringing, and circumstances all seem to have conspired, in fact, to focus the attention of Americans on this earth."[37] Indeed, individual independence is

---

34. Tocqueville, *Democracy in America*, 507.
35. Tocqueville, *Democracy in America*, 622.
36. Tocqueville, *Democracy in America*, 621.
37. Tocqueville, *Democracy in America*, 518.

the most dangerous threat to religion.[38] Individualism shapes the church in many ways, but one of the most important is that "it always takes effort for such men to tear themselves away from their private affairs in order to take up common ones. Their natural inclination is to leave common affairs in the charge of the sole visible and permanent representative of collective interests, which is the state."[39] In the church, however, it means that the church staff does the church work because Bourgeois Christians won't, or the 10 percent do the work while the 90 percent watch and listen.

Furthermore, and unfortunately, some churches elect utilitarian individualists to leadership positions, not because of their work in the kingdom of God, but because of their success in the mammon world. But they can't lead church members out of the wilderness of individualism because the bog of the work world holds them fast. As Nietzsche explains: "And that it is therefore the modern, noisy, time-consuming, self-congratulatory, stupidly proud work ethic more than anything else that trains and prepares us for a 'lack of faith'?"[40] Too many evangelical churches suffer from leadership failures for this reason and others. Now back to Tocqueville. Is he out of date?

To brush off Tocqueville's argument against individualism, one might say: "So what, that was a long time ago, and we have made great progress." But consider what some twentieth-century philosophers say about individualism. Hannah Arendt explains that one of modern philosophy's main contributions "has been an exclusive concern with the self, as distinguished from the soul or person or man in general, an attempt to reduce all experiences, with the world as well as with other human beings, to experiences between man and himself."[41] Likewise, Charles Taylor calls individualism one of the three malaises of modernity.[42]

German Existentialist Karl Jaspers, writing in the mid-twentieth century, says that civilization is disintegrating: "In all past history there was a self-evident bond between man and man. . . . The most visible sign of today's disintegration is that more and more men do not understand one another, . . . that they are indifferent to one another, that there is no longer any reliable community or loyalty."[43] This is the fragmentation

---

38. Tocqueville, *Democracy in America*, 509.
39. Tocqueville, *Democracy in America*, 793.
40. Nietzsche, *Beyond Good and Evil*, 51.
41. Arendt, *Human Condition*, 254.
42. Taylor, *Ethics of Authenticity*, 2.
43. Jaspers, *Way to Wisdom*, 25.

and social isolation of individualism. And sociologist Philip Rieff agrees: "Crowded more and more together, we are learning to live more distantly from one another."[44] Likewise, another twentieth-century philosopher, Theodor Adorno, describes the individualism of classical liberalism as "the truly bourgeois principle."[45] It is competitive and guided by the self-centered "let me be," "let me get ahead." (In part, this is why "bourgeois" is in the title of this book.)

Very succinctly, Adorno attacks classical liberalism, and classical liberalism is one anchor of Bourgeois Christianity and the individualist ethics that oppose Christian ethics. Classical liberalism is written into the Declaration of Independence and follows John Locke's *Second Treatise on Government*, and this self-oriented and self-centered ethic is embedded in the hearts of many Americans.[46] This is the cultural model of possessive individualism. Possessive individualism operates on the principle that "the individual's freedom is rightly limited only by the requirements of others' freedom. The individual is proprietor of his own person, for which he owes nothing to society."[47] But the Bible teaches that Christians owe much to their neighbors.

I end the chapter with this thought: Evangelicals live in the iPod, iPad, iPhone world but never recognize the I-Me-My focus of contemporary Evangelicalism that leads to a shirking-duty kind of piety. It is an age in which the saints are a football team. And however far Evangelicals are theologically from the liberal denominations, existentially they live next door in the Christian me-world neighborhood where the doors are closed and the windows shut. Religious liberalism, deeply imbued with the me focus of Romanticism and its subjectivity, is the religious me without the evangelical biblespeak and theology.

And for reasons that I will explain later, me-ness is okay for Evangelicals as long as they have orthodox theology, go to church, and vote Republican. Consequently, many Evangelicals can't imagine that God's "wonderful plan" for their lives means denying themselves, taking up crosses, and following Jesus. Or that in carrying out the plan, they need to wear the full

---

44. Rieff, *Triumph of the Therapeutic*, 208.

45. Adorno, *Minima Moralia*, 27.

46. See Goldwin, talking about Locke's *Second Treatise*: "Locke . . . does not explicitly deny the importance of excellence or love; he simply disregards them. For that matter, he barely uses or does not use at all, in the *Second Treatise*, such words as *charity, soul, ethics, morality, virtue, noble,* or *love*" ("John Locke," 459). Emphasis in original.

47. Macpherson, *Possessive Individualism*, 269.

armor of God and be armed like a Roman soldier to fight the good fight of faith. Bourgeois Christians want to win the crown without first carrying the cross. Seven times in the book of Revelation Jesus says that you must be an overcomer, a conqueror like he was, to sit on the throne with him.[48]

It is easy to skate on the smooth ice of the world but hard to climb a mountain with Christ. And as long as Evangelicals see moral relativism and wokeism as the great evils of the age and not the me-centered individualism that operates in most evangelical churches, their churches have little chance of avoiding the seduction of individualism.

---

48. See generally Rev 2–3 in the NASB and the ESV.

Chapter 2 Democracy in America Revisited: Habits of the Heart

IN 1983 ROBERT N. Bellah and several colleagues wrote *Habits of the Heart* after studying contemporary American individualism, and Tocqueville influenced their work. They focused their sociological study on how social mores, or what Tocqueville calls habits of the heart, affect contemporary individualism, and how individualism's ethos can undermine culture. Indeed, they feared that American individualism had become cancerous.[1] This social malignancy arises in part from the ethos of individualism that "seems more than ever determined to press ahead with the task of letting go of all criteria other than radical private validation."[2] This ends in the radical autonomy of an improvisational self.[3]

As the authors explain, individualism underwrites the core of American society,[4] and it produces "a way of life that is neither individually nor socially viable."[5] It is not viable because we are social creatures and need society, companionship, and love. Consistent with this failure, Bellah et al. describe individualism as the belief that the individual is the primary reality and that society is of a second order, a kind of artificial construct.[6] French sociologist Louis Dumont similarly explains that individualism valorizes

---

1. Bellah et al., *Habits of the Heart*, vii.
2. Bellah et al., *Habits of the Heart*, 79.
3. Bellah et al., *Habits of the Heart*, 81.
4. Bellah et al., *Habits of the Heart*, 142.
5. Bellah et al., *Habits of the Heart*, 144.
6. Bellah et al., *Habits of the Heart*, 334.

the individual and neglects or subordinates the social whole.[7] Bellah et al. expand and deepen Tocqueville's analysis of contemporary individualism by describing two types of individualism.

The first type is *utilitarian individualism*, and these individuals devote themselves to success, career, achievement, creating wealth, exercising self-control, and being willing to sacrifice to get ahead. The utilitarian individual's goal is to advance beyond peers by applying initiative and using talents. This leads to a calculating pursuit of their material interests, and self-improvement and self-advancement become goals.[8] Utilitarian individuals seek their "separate identity in the exercise of [their] own growing powers, ever freer of restraint by others and ever farther out in front of them."[9]

This sounds like the style of individualism that Tocqueville describes—people devoted to getting ahead and clamoring for success. For Bellah, Benjamin Franklin and his *Poor Richard's Almanac* represent this practical type of individualism with advice like: "Early to bed and early to rise, makes a man healthy, wealthy, and wise."[10] In Bourgeois Christian circles, the utilitarian individual is often the person who believes that God has called him or her to make money and who pushes ever harder for success. They baptize their personal goals and their work, they sweat in the kingdom of mammon, and they coast in the kingdom of God. These people rarely have time to love their neighbor. Indeed, they may use their neighbors to get ahead.

Bellah et al. call the second type of individualism *expressive individualism*. In part, it reacts against utilitarian individualism's grasping for material gain. Expressive individualism strives to cultivate the self more deeply, rather than earn money and gain success. Walt Whitman's *Leaves of Grass* represents this type of individualism with the idea that I celebrate myself.[11] Whitman celebrates the body, sensuality, and sexual gratification, and his type of individualism is grounded in human subjectivity, feeling, and sentiment. For Whitman the goal is to cultivate and express the self.[12] More importantly, expressive individuals tend to isolate

---

7. Dumont, *Essays on Individualism*, 25.
8. Bellah et al., *Habits of the Heart*, 33.
9. Bellah et al., *Habits of the Heart*, 68–69.
10. Bellah et al., *Habits of the Heart*, 32.
11. Bellah et al., *Habits of the Heart*, 34.
12. Bellah et al., *Habits of the Heart*, 35.

themselves into lifestyle enclaves of people with similar interests and tastes, but these enclaves are not moral communities.[13] Lifestyle enclaves celebrate "the narcissism of similarity."[14]

Ethics for the expressive individualist becomes getting what you want and enjoying it. "Utility replaces duty; self-expression unseats authority. 'Being good' becomes 'feeling good.'"[15] And as I will show later, many expressive individuals have mutated into twenty-first-century therapeutic selves and helped create our therapeutic society that discounts religion and personal responsibility.

The authors further explain how expressive individualism's influence has increased at religion's expense:

> When science seemed to have dominated the explanatory schemas of the external world, morality and religion took refuge in human subjectivity, in feeling and sentiment. Morality and religion were related to aesthetics, the realm of feeling par excellence, . . . [and] with the emergence of psychology as an academic field—and, even more important, as a form of popular discourse . . . the purely subjective grounding of expressive individualism became complete.[16]

"Purely subjective grounding" means that the individual decides what matters in life, what is true, and what is real. These individuals do not base life decisions on the Christian Bible, Platonic forms, Aristotelian nature, natural law, or anything else primordial. For modern people, "the highest ideal is the 'self' itself."[17]

There is no first order, no arche, no logos, no natural law, and no human nature. Hence there is no defense against nihilism. There is only flux, and when only flux exists, only nothingness remains. All that is left is the emptiness of values, but the individualist cannot recognize the emptiness of the radical, private validation of the improvisational self. And as Bellah et al. explain in talking about Evangelicals, "the tendency of contemporary American life is to pull all of us into lifestyle enclaves of one sort or another."[18] Enclaves, however, are not covenantal relationships.

---

13. Bellah et al., *Habits of the Heart*, 71.
14. Bellah et al., *Habits of the Heart*, 72.
15. Bellah et al., *Habits of the Heart*, 77.
16. Bellah et al., *Habits of the Heart*, 46.
17. Gardner, "Eros and Ambitions," 233.
18. Bellah et al., *Habits of the Heart*, 74.

It helps to understand what the authors mean in the long passage just quoted. First, the rise of modern science replaced the biblical creation account of the world and the universe. This, along with other influences, ended the dominant religious view of the medieval age and made Christianity less credible in an increasingly secular age. As the credibility of Christianity declined and secularization increased, the influence of Christian morality and teaching also declined. This led, in part, to the aesthetic replacing the ethical and to private thoughts replacing public duties in a secular age.

But secularization offers no transcendent or unchanging basis for truth, with the result that, as Nietzsche says, "God is dead," which is not a theological fact for him but rather a sociological or cultural fact.[19] When God is dead, that leaves pragmatism, historicism, absurdism, utilitarianism, or nihilism, all of which share the view that there is no ultimate truth. But don't be mistaken. A secular, individualistic culture does not want ultimate truth. Truth and tradition hinder personal freedom. Individualists want to invent their own truth, but that leaves them with nothing more than mere opinion or in philosophical terms—the abyss.

This is why Bellah describes contemporary American individualism as characterized by a radical autonomy that produces an improvisational self—a plastic self conjured up out of feelings with no signposts, guidelines, or boundaries. Evangelicals pounce on this as moral relativism, but they don't see that undergirding the moral relativism is the aesthetic approach to life. So while denouncing moral relativism, Bourgeois Christians embrace the aesthetic and an easy religion that focuses on well-being and follows the age.

Of course, both utilitarian and expressive individualism focus on the self, and both versions involve withdrawing into the self. The utilitarian individual strives for success and achievement; the expressive individual focuses on feelings, sentiments, and how the inner self is doing. Bellah et al. also identify important social forces other than individualism that have an atomistic effect on culture. These forces developed in the twentieth century.

First, life has become separated into "functional sectors: home and workplace, work and leisure, white collar and blue collar, public and private."[20] These divisions lead to seeing the problems and successes of life as individual in nature and things to be balanced within the various sectors.

---

19. Nietzsche, *Gay Science*, 181.
20. Bellah et al., *Habits of the Heart*, 43.

Public and private roles contrast sharply, and this leads to individuals having public lives and separate private lives without community.

In the religious sphere, this promotes a privatized spirituality focused on a believer's inner life rather than the broader life of the daily world where privatized religion makes few public appearances, and neighbors live in the public world. Someone can go to church every Sunday, pray every morning, and read the Bible every day, and have nothing more than a privatized religion, yet believe they are very spiritual. And they believe this because they have been taught that this is spirituality. They have no sense of a covenantal community, neighbor duty, or working in God's kingdom. And without the ethical element, these privatized religious exercises often end in little more than a spiritualized, expressive individualism. The aesthete lives a private existence.

Second, developments in the field of psychology, and especially the rise of popular psychology, have enhanced expressive individualism's role in society. I call this the rise and dominance of the therapeutic culture. And when you add to the therapeutic mentality a corporate economy, a bureaucratized government, and a consumerist market, you promote an expressivist individualism that, as Bellah et al. explain, lives "for the liberation and fulfillment of the individual. Its genius is that it enables the individual to think of commitments—from marriage and work to political and religious involvement—as enhancements of the sense of individual well-being rather than as moral imperatives."[21] And now we are back to Tocqueville and the American goal of well-being.

The aesthetic replaces the ethical, and this is a sign of the times.[22] Personality has replaced character. The self relishes self-expression and self-fulfillment but avoids self-denial for a higher purpose.[23] The aesthete wants to be pleased, and a Bourgeois Christian aesthete can find a good sermon very pleasing. As sociologist Robert Wuthnow, an expert on American Evangelicals, notes: "If we [Evangelicals] go to church, we want to hear sweet sermons on the blessings of life, not something that will make us squirm in our seats. We want to be reassured that all will be well as long as we believe in God and give token amounts to the work of the church."[24] This is the aesthetic approach to spirituality. The moral

---

21. Bellah et al., *Habits of the Heart*, 47.
22. Jacobs, *Visit to Vanity Fair*, 164.
23. Stivers, *Shades of Loneliness*, 13.
24. Wuthnow, *Crisis in the Churches*, 228.

imperatives of loving God and loving one's neighbor become artifacts of a lost age. Most Americans, including many Evangelicals, do not see loving their neighbor as a strategy for self-fulfillment or a way to improve their well-being. God is no longer sovereign; the self is.

This bureaucratized and therapeutic culture of self-fulfillment directs individuals "to make of [their] particular segment of life a small world of its own."[25] It becomes an enclave. And again, we are back to what Tocqueville describes as an isolating individualism brought up to date late in the twentieth century. As Bellah et al. make clear, most Americans believe they are "an autonomous self existing independently, entirely outside any tradition and community."[26] But they deny Americans' autonomy because they understand how culture destroys the individual's power to determine the self. It follows that in seeking autonomy, Bourgeois Christians fall outside the covenantal community yet offer enough biblespeak and church attendance to show they are saved. Although soothing, it is not spiritual, but it fits well in the therapeutic culture.

So the therapeutic culture, influenced by individualism, promotes the therapeutic attitude that emphasizes independence and autonomy and de-emphasizes personal responsibility. This attitude begins with the self and strives to be independent of others and includes being independent of other people's standards or, for that matter, any standards. This kind of therapeutic self-actualizing crushes self-sacrifice.[27] But it is not just expressive individualism that promotes independence and avoids community.

Many contemporary Evangelicals follow the individualistic ideas of John Locke's classical liberalism. His philosophy deeply influenced the Founding Fathers, and that influence continues, especially among white, Anglo-Saxon Protestants. Classical liberalism is neither covenantal nor community focused; the only body that matters is the individual's body, not a communal or covenantal body like Christ's church. And as the French liberal Benjamin Constant declares: "Our freedom must consist of peaceful enjoyment and private independence.... The aim of the moderns is the enjoyment of security in private pleasures; and they call liberty the guarantees

---

25. Bellah et al., *Habits of the Heart*, 50.

26. Bellah et al., *Habits of the Heart*, 65.

27. Bellah et al., *Habits of the Heart*, 100. The authors explain: "In its pure form, the therapeutic attitude denies all forms of obligation and commitment in relationships, replacing them only with the ideal of full, open, honest communication among self-actualized individuals.... For therapeutically liberated individuals, obligation of any kind becomes problematic in relationships" (101).

accorded by institutions to these pleasures."[28] This is the classical liberal ideal for life. It fits nicely with a privatized religion.

In one sense, classical individualism claims the freedom to be left alone, but with that also comes being alone and leaving others alone.[29] There is a certain folly in this self-styled autonomy and independence. As Bellah et al. explain: "The irony is that here, too, just where we think we are most free, we are most coerced by the dominant beliefs of our own culture. For it is a powerful cultural fiction that we not only can, but must, make up our deepest beliefs in the isolation of our private selves."[30] As such, the claim to autonomy often hides the individual's social conformity. But the pseudo-autonomy of classical liberalism is often the Bourgeois Christian's way to utilitarian individualism.

This individualistic, non-covenantal thinking undermines the kingdom of God and rests on worldly political philosophy, not the Bible. Likewise, the therapeutic attitude that the community is or should be designed to satisfy personal needs is not the biblical model; indeed, it contravenes that model. Both pagan and evangelical individualists find their model within themselves and express it in their feelings.[31] But the apostle Paul makes it clear:

> For even as the body is one and yet has many members, and all the members of the body, though they are many, are one body, so also is Christ. For by one Spirit we were all baptized into one body, whether Jews or Greeks, whether slaves or free, and we were all made to drink of one Spirit. For the body is not one member, but many. (1 Cor 12:12–14)

The Bible teaches that true equality is based in God's love. It teaches the unity of community. It also teaches the importance of the body and the body of the church united.

This is holism, not individualism. Holism valorizes the social whole, the church, and, in a sense, makes the neighbor transcendent. There is no place for this me-first kind of "I gotta be free, I gotta be me" individualism. But the thin theology of American evangelism has led many to believe that salvation is all about me and God's wonderful plan for my life, when it is in fact about us, with the me being only part of an us called the body of Christ.

28. Constant, *Liberty of Ancients*, para. 25.
29. Bellah et al., *Habits of the Heart*, 23.
30. Bellah et al., *Habits of the Heart*, 65.
31. Taylor, *Ethics of Authenticity*, 29.

Professor Wells describes the corrupt evangelical outlook well: "We imagine that the great purposes of life are realized in the improvement of our own private inner disposition. We imagine that for those who love God and are called according to his purpose, all things work together for their satisfaction and the inner tranquility of their lives."[32] For Bourgeois Christians, God was created for them, while the Bible says that they are created for God. Too many Evangelicals recline in the well-being and expressive individualism of the age. This is worldly. Worldliness means living in the wrong culture except on Sundays. Worldliness is being double minded, and a double-minded person is unstable (Jas 1:8).

So here is the contemporary, anti-Christian culture: the self has replaced the soul, the therapist has replaced the pastor, the good life has replaced the gospel, self-fulfillment has replaced self-denial, the aesthetic has replaced the ethical, and the secular spirit rules the age. In other words, egoism rules. This creates a cultural vertigo that keeps most Evangelicals too dizzy to think of anyone but themselves, while tripping and spinning ever deeper into paganism. They are caught in a worldly maelstrom but don't know it.

---

32. Wells, *God in the Wasteland*, 114–15.

Chapter 3 The Therapeutic Culture: The Age of Self-Fulfillment, Sickness, and the Psyche

IN THE LAST TWO chapters, I described individualism and its prejudice against the neighbor and community. I now dig further into the age to explain our therapeutic culture and to describe Philip Rieff's "psychological man." This chapter shows the fundamentals of the therapeutic culture and the characteristics of psychological man and the contemporary focus on the psyche. It describes how cultural forces produce character ideals and impose worldviews and shows the difference between the Christian and the psychological man that the therapeutic culture breeds.[1] The seeds of an individualistic democracy, especially expressive individualism, have produced, in part, our therapeutic culture.

This chapter begins with sociologist Philip Rieff's work on the therapeutic society and the psychological man. As Rieff explains, the modern age arose out of the destruction of traditional and classical communities.[2] In other words, much of modern-age thought and culture has sought to destroy Christianity as a cultural power and way of understanding reality. (See Friedrich Nietzsche's *On the Genealogy of Morality* for an example of this approach.) Rieff describes the culture's power and control over people.

According to Rieff, "Culture is another name for a design of motives directing the self outward, toward those communal purposes in which

---

1. I use the term "psychological man" without gender distinctions to describe Philip Rieff's concept throughout this chapter. I use it as a term of art, Philip Rieff's art.

2. Rieff, *Triumph of the Therapeutic*, 57.

alone the self can be realized and satisfied."[3] Everyone lives in a sociological system called culture that has communal or group purposes that structure life, and cultures direct the self outward into the community. These structures create motives, goals, reasons for living, and guides for behavior, and we live satisfying lives by undertaking the communal purposes. A culture also frames an understanding of reality and life. Cultures that existed before the therapeutic culture have imposed moral demand systems.[4] These moral systems prescribe what to do and what not to do, how to live and how not to live.

True Christian culture imposes moral demands. "You shall be My people, And I will be your God" structures the Christian life (Jer 30:22). Or as the Westminster Shorter Catechism teaches: "Man's chief end is to glorify God, and to enjoy him forever."[5] This declares the motive, goal, and reason for living. The Christian culture also commands rules for living like the Ten Commandments, the Proverbs, and Jesus's and Paul's teachings, which impose "thou shalts" and "thou shalt nots." They describe the way of wisdom and condemn the way of folly. Loving the neighbor is both a goal and a rule for living. But more importantly, it is central to the communal purpose commanded by God and a way that God blesses Christians and others. It is the way of joy. Finally, the Christian culture has a model for how to live, and that model is Jesus Christ.

Jesus's self-sacrifice and his teaching direct life to the communal purposes summarized in the Great Commandment: love God, love neighbor. Christianity gave meaning to life for people in the early church and the medieval world based on a framework of a righteous and omnipotent God, the creation, good and evil, and heaven and hell. The Bible presents the foundations for life in God's redemptive plan.

On the other hand, Rieff describes how modernity's therapeutic culture has replaced Christian culture with the goal of releasing people to indulge their appetites and seek fulfillment. But the therapeutic culture offers no narrative by which to integrate life and give it purpose and meaning. If it has an ethic, the ethic is to focus on self and personal well-being—the ethics of egoism. Egoism is freedom without responsibility. This follows Tocqueville's description of life in democracy as equality of conditions.

3. Rieff, *Triumph of the Therapeutic*, 3.
4. Rieff, *Triumph of the Therapeutic*, 211.
5. See "The Shorter Catechism," question 1, "What is the chief end of man?," in Committee for Christian Education & Publications, *Westminster Confession of Faith*, 3.

Rieff describes this new, therapeutic culture as anti-Christian, anti-tradition, pro-instinct, and pro-desire because the idea of human perfection has changed the traditional understanding of evil and immorality.[6] It is therapeutic because it works to enhance people's sense of well-being, especially for the needs of their psyches. It creates a negative community or a community without a unity of interest, which frees people to focus on themselves.[7] So the instinct control of the Christian "thou shalt nots" and the fear of God have lost place to uncontrolled freedom and the sexual license of the exalted self and its fragile psyche.

As Rieff explains, however, the Christian ethic pushes individuals into a communal purpose and away from the self. He uses the example of Moses in the wilderness: "I suspect the children of Israel did not spend much time elaborating a doctrine of the golden calf; they naively danced around it, until Moses . . . [stopped the fun] . . . and insisted on civilizing them, by submerging their individualities within a communal purpose."[8] Christianity redirects the natural instincts of self-worship and the passion for liberation into the biblical goals of serving God and loving neighbor. For psychological man and the therapeutic culture, the Christian culture represses individual desires by commanding followers to renounce them. For example, "don't commit adultery" is a biblical, moralizing demand. "Gratify your desires" is a therapeutic culture release. God's law represses; the therapeutic culture releases. And here is where faith plays the essential role.

By faith Christians obey because they fear God or love God or both. His commands redirect their instinctual energies and desires into kingdom work. Most importantly, they are a blessing and a benefit for fullness of life, not draconian rules. The narrow way is the blessed way. God offers believers an abundant life in his kingdom project of redemption that includes peace, beauty, joy, and justice.

Psychological man scorns this as oppressive and antihuman and has faith that there is no god, or at least no god of judgment and righteousness. He wants to avoid attachment to any particular meaning in life and to other people unless they enhance his sense of well-being or soothe his psyche.[9] Therapeutic detachment defeats neighbor love, and saving the self comes

---

6. Rieff, *Triumph of the Therapeutic*, 6.
7. Rieff, *Triumph of the Therapeutic*, 25.
8. Rieff, *Triumph of the Therapeutic*, 7.
9. Rieff, *Triumph of the Therapeutic*, 50.

from fulfilling the self, not from serving God. Indeed, for psychological man, salvation is obsolete, except for being one's own savior.[10]

Moreover, psychological man doesn't need eternal salvation; he wants to save himself through autonomy and freedom from the restraints of communal purposes. He wants to be his own god. Psychological man views religious cultures as guilt cultures that limit behaviors and experimenting in life.[11] Guilt tends to subordinate the self to communal purposes, which require attachments. For psychological man, natural drives and self-focus are good, not sinful. And while the religious culture tries to control impulses, the therapeutic culture encourages them. Consequently, the therapeutic culture of self-expression and self-fulfillment has dumped religious commands into the cul-de-sac of history while racing down the freeway of a psychologized goal of well-being.

Indeed, the therapeutic society has become the "Live and let live," "I'm okay, you're okay," and "If it feels good, do it!" world of self-actualization, and American society operates as a culture of release. It releases individuals from God's control in the religious order. It releases instinctual passions, and it opens the dikes to the materialism of technology's abundance. Consumption is king; devotion to something other than self is heretical. With the new piety of the self, comfort is the salve for empty souls—no more balm in Gilead. Comfort comes from drugs, therapy, consumption, sex, and entertainment, all part of an aesthetic salvation. Having more and enjoying more become the way to overcome the psychic pain of living alone, even when you are living with others.

Consequently, the therapeutic displaces the biblical command to serve God in a life directed to communal purposes, because the therapeutic society has no communal purposes. And as Rieff explains: "Religious man was born to be saved; psychological man is born to be pleased."[12] As a result, the therapeutic culture shifts from controlling to releasing, from a community interest—the kingdom of God—to releasing the individual for pleasure seeking in their little kingdom of one. Psychological man strives to overcome religion's repression of instinct, and the therapeutic culture applauds him along his way. A simple example shows how this works.

A twentieth-century British intellectual, Aldous Huxley, explains this releasing activity concisely—how he didn't like the old religious morality

---

10. Rieff, *Triumph of the Therapeutic*, 10.
11. Furedi, *Therapy Culture*, 33.
12. Rieff, *Triumph of the Therapeutic*, 19.

because it interfered with his sexual desires and how he defeated those controls to gratify his desires:

> For myself, as, no doubt, for most of my contemporaries, the philosophy of meaninglessness [nihilism] was essentially an instrument of liberation. The liberation we desired was simultaneously liberation from a certain political and economic system and liberation from a certain system of morality. We objected to the morality because it interfered with our sexual freedom; we objected to the political and economic system because it was unjust. The supporters of these systems claimed that in some way they embodied the meaning (a Christian meaning, they insisted) of the world. There was one admirably simple method of confuting these people and at the same time justifying ourselves in our political and erotic revolt: we could deny that the world had any meaning whatsoever.[13]

Huxley wanted sexual freedom, and Christian morality restricted that freedom to the marriage bed, so he voted for nothingness, or nihilism, against the Christian God. Nothingness released him to erotic revolt and sensual pleasure. The desire for freedom from communal purposes and communal ethics led to religion's decline in the modern age. The secular religion of therapeutic self-worship and self-focus replaced the Christian religion of self-control and self-sacrifice.

But Rieff is not the only scholar to describe religion's decline. In *The Disenchantment of the World*, contemporary French philosopher Marcel Gauchet argues that around 1700, Christian history came to a halt.[14] In other words, the Christian religion, based on the Bible and Christ's work, no longer structures Western culture or instills core beliefs. The organizing vision of the "human-social phenomenon" that individualism promotes replaced Christianity's organizing vision.[15] Gauchet is not talking about personal religious belief, which continues today. He is describing how a secular and individualistic understanding of life has replaced a biblical understanding. This is another way of saying that God is dead.

Importantly, Gauchet describes how religion's decline has transformed individual piety. The decline among believers is in the poverty of their practices, not in their thoughts. In other words, religious practices have declined,

---

13. Huxley, *Ends and Means*, 273.
14. Gauchet, *Disenchantment of the World*, 162.
15. Gauchet, *Disenchantment of the World*, 94.

not religious thinking. As Gauchet explains: "What matters is not what the members of a given society personally think and believe, but the pattern of their thought processes, their mode of coexistence, the form of their integration with being and the dynamics of their actions."[16]

Accordingly, what Christians believe is not the key to religious devotion. Thoughts directed to action, practices of living with others, and working in communities are the fruits robust religion produces and what a moribund religion lacks. In fact, Gauchet says people can be believers but not religious. And as he notes about contemporary Christianity, "All that remains of it today are individual experiences and belief systems."[17]

These individual experiences are predominately aesthetic experiences bereft of the ethical. And now we are back to the neap tide of the evangelical knowledge culture with its pride of Bible knowledge and poverty of loving action. But Christianity is fundamentally existential and, therefore, foremost about practices of living, and that is why the Bible describes the Christian life with verbs like walking, striving, fighting, and serving.

Consistent with what Gauchet describes as decline, many Bourgeois Christians don't walk, strive, fight, or serve, but they focus instead on learning belief systems and worldviews and enjoying the aesthetic pleasures they bring. For many dispensationalists, Christianity is a belief system about the rapture and the ages and stages of God's redemptive plan. Likewise, the neo-Calvinists emphasize a belief system based in the Westminster Confession of Faith and preach strong doctrine.

But evangelical knowledge cultures depersonalize and decontextualize Christianity, which the Bible never does. The Bible always describes people acting in a social context: Moses in Egypt asking Pharaoh to let the children of Israel go, Jeremiah in Jerusalem prophesying the Judeans's doom, and Paul in Athens explaining the faith to King Agrippa. The Christian knowledge culture withers Christianity down to a system of knowledge aesthetically understood. It follows the therapeutic age and Christianity's decline as it turns the Christian ethical culture into a release culture. Indeed, Christianity is not about the gospel well understood; it is about the gospel well lived. One can't embrace the creed but ignore the deed. And the therapeutic goal of self-fulfillment hinders Bourgeois Christians in other ways.

British sociologist Frank Furedi argues that the therapeutic culture's shift of focus from the social group to the individual's internal life has

16. Gauchet, *Disenchantment of the World*, 101.
17. Gauchet, *Disenchantment of the World*, 101.

reoriented intellectual life towards a preoccupied self. Part 2 of this book describes the consciousness focus of the modern age and how it produces Bourgeois Christians. I call this the Cartesian consciousness of Bourgeois Christianity. In part, preoccupation with the self follows the psyche focus of the therapeutic culture and leads to a Christian intellectualism. That kind of intellectualism focuses on belief systems, and as Gauchet explains, that is what is left in the age of religion's demise—mostly thinking about religion, not doing it.

Furthermore, this reorienting from the community to the self turns believers away from the neighbor and Christ's communal purposes. Furedi explains that this "one-dimensional preoccupation with the self often leads to overlooking the social and cultural foundations of individual identity."[18] Bourgeois Christians ignore the Christian duty to neighbor and to God's kingdom plan. They don't recognize their identities as God's children and workers in his kingdom. But St. Paul understood his identity in Christ well. He was God's slave charged to evangelize the gentiles. This was part of his social and communal identity within the body of Christ.

Furedi, an insightful critic of the therapeutic culture, says that "it is important to realise that the therapeutically constructed self is one that is unencumbered by the obligations that are demanded by intimates in the private sphere. That is why the affirmation of the therapeutic self represents an estrangement not only from public life, but also the private sphere."[19] In the age of therapy and nihilism, psychological man is usually on the verge of becoming nothing, and Bourgeois Christians are usually on the verge of doing nothing.

Why? Because Bourgeois Christians detach themselves and seek release from communal purposes that demand time and effort. They privatize Christianity. Loving neighbors engages both public and private spheres, and even before the rise of the therapeutic society, Tocqueville had already described the isolating effects of individualism. The therapeutic has accelerated the fragmentation that individualism began. Moreover, the Christian knowledge culture lets one withdraw into self and focus on consciousness—more learning, not more loving.

Indeed, the therapeutic culture sneaks in the front door of evangelical churches in paradoxical ways, including preaching. Therapy can

---

18. Furedi, *Therapy Culture*, 25.
19. Furedi, *Therapy Culture*, 73.

be informative and not transformative, but biblical teaching should transform.[20] Therapy's goal is to help people understand themselves better, to recognize the importance of their feelings, and to make them feel better about themselves. Exegetical preaching becomes therapeutic when it makes those sitting in the pews feel spiritual but does not change lives. It releases them to return to their bourgeois lifestyles.

The classic example of this is the "downtown church" where the pastor preaches strong sermons every Sunday but demands little of his congregation. Members of these churches become connoisseurs of sermons, not ambassadors for Christ, and the aesthetic of the knowledge culture replaces the ethic of the covenant. This has a therapeutic effect on Bourgeois Christians, who would likely claim that calling them to work is legalism.

But the ethical is not legalism. The ethical is Jesus's call to love the neighbor whenever opportunities arise. Paradoxically, the knowledge culture is legalism, especially the theological correctness of the knowledge culture. Whereas we commonly think of legalism as a do-this-and-don't-do-that kind of religion to make God happy, the knowledge culture legalism is think this and don't think that, and God will be happy with you.

In fact, legalism is giving the law less than it requires, and Jesus the lawgiver says to love your neighbor. Notably, R. C. Sproul describes the legalist as one who "is not so much seeking to obey God or honor Christ as he is to obey rules that are devoid of any personal relationship."[21] In other words, what is in the mind becomes external to the existential call of God, which is a call to action. The prophetic voice is a command to change your life's direction and goals.

Indeed, without the prophetic claims, preaching turns therapeutic and aesthetic and fails to ignite the spirit to love. The old call to ascetic forbearance of desires—daily taking up of the cross—becomes aesthetic information that comforts the hearers and enhances their sense of well-being because they hear a good sermon. If they enjoy the sermon, they give the preacher an A. But as in the parable of the sower, the seed sown among the thorns of the third soil represents those who hear the word, but the worry of the world and the deceitfulness of riches make these hearers unfruitful. And in the therapeutic age, the thorns of well-being and self-fulfillment, those worldly cares blighting evangelical circles, render many hearers unfruitful (Matt 13:18–23).

20. Rieff, *Triumph of the Therapeutic*, 64.
21. Sproul, "3 Types of Legalism," para. 3.

Evangelicals live in the age of the dizzy consumer who is drowning in advertising, Hollywood glitter, self-help books, spa facials, Oprah, *The Bachelor* and *The Bachelorette*, the cosmo and the vesper, organic bananas, lattes, online love affairs, Facebook, X (formerly Twitter), TikTok, and selfies. Many Evangelicals think that the culture does not control them because they believe in the Bible; however, our high-speed culture drives them to seek self-fulfillment. But there is more to the therapeutic: seeking to soothe us, the therapeutic culture diagnoses us as sick, and sick people think about themselves and their problems, not their neighbor.

In 1787 the great German writer Goethe concluded, "I . . . believe that humanity will win in the long run; I am only afraid that at the same time the world will have turned into one huge hospital where everyone is everybody else's humane nurse."[22] How prophetic! The hospital has happened in America and in the evangelical church. According to one prominent evangelical preacher, Christians are God's workmanship created in Christ Jesus for good therapy and not good works. The kingdom of God has become a hospital, and convalescing Christians have few Christian duties except to be treated by God, the great therapist.[23] But I've never seen a convalescent carry a cross every day, fight a good fight, run a race before a great cloud of witnesses, or wear armor. And as Eva S. Moskowitz explains, "We live in an age consumed by worship of the psyche . . . bound together by a gospel of psychological happiness."[24] But it is actually the age of vast psychological unhappiness, commonly diagnosed as sickness of the psyche, and to enjoy psychological happiness, therapists and drugs must cure psychological sickness.

In her book *In Therapy We Trust: America's Obsession with Self-Fulfillment*, Moskowitz describes the three tenets of the therapeutic gospel. First, according to this new gospel, our supreme goal should be happiness, and we should measure our success with a psychological yardstick. Second, our problems come from psychological causes, rather than political, economic, or educational causes. Third, we can treat our psychological problems.[25] And underlying these ideas is that psychological problems make us sick.

---

22. Goethe, *Italian Journey*, 317.

23. Piper, "Don't Serve God." Piper tells us that God is not looking for assistants, and the gospel is not a call to Christian service: "God is not looking for people to work for him," because "Christianity is fundamentally convalescence" (paras. 2, 7).

24. Moskowitz, *In Therapy We Trust*, 1.

25. Moskowitz, *In Therapy We Trust*, 2–3.

No doubt many people suffer from serious psychological illnesses and need care. This chapter does not dismiss those needs nor contend that they don't exist. This chapter describes the cultural problems that the therapeutic culture creates, not mental illnesses that need treatment. So what other problems does the therapeutic raise for Evangelicals?

Moskowitz describes the problem with the therapeutic morality: "This therapeutic morality . . . focuses our attention on the private life, blinding us to the larger, public good."[26] The therapeutic culture takes social and economic problems and psychologizes them, which hinders the cure. Because of the psychological emphasis, the individual's mind or psyche is the issue, and this follows the age of the Cartesian consciousness that focuses on the mind. But overdiagnosing mental health problems increases the number of people who think they are sick, and sick people focus on themselves. This is part of the therapeutic culture.

Finally, as Rieff explains, the death of a culture begins when that culture can no longer "communicate ideals in ways that remain inwardly compelling."[27] A Christian knowledge culture fails to communicate the ideals and unity of Christianity in a compelling way. People won't sacrifice for correct theology, better doctrine, or beautiful preaching when it is all understood aesthetically and not existentially. It sounds good, it feels good, but it breeds Bourgeois Christians. The next chapter describes how this works out in the churches. I call it the thin theology of American revivalism.

---

26. Moskowitz, *In Therapy We Trust*, 7.
27. Rieff, *Triumph of the Therapeutic*, 14.

Chapter 4 Evangelical Populism and the Thin Theology of American Revivalism

THIS CHAPTER DESCRIBES THE shallow theology found in many evangelical churches, even in churches that teach the robust theology that Professor Wells urges. This is another paradox. In other words, this shallowness exists in believers' lives even when pastors preach biblical sermons every week and even in denominations known for their theology. The paradox is that shallow teaching blunts the deep teaching. Specifically, the theology of American revivalism stunts the understanding of duty because the framework of Bourgeois Christianity is the thin theology of revivalism. This shallow teaching controls the understanding of what it means to be a Christian for many Evangelicals.

Some popular evangelistic techniques disenchant the word of God and rely on a populist view of Scripture. In other words, these techniques level or preempt essential truth, and biblical half-truths are untruths. Furthermore, worldly Evangelicals make Christianity attractive in ways unfaithful to Scripture. We can understand this thin theology in substantial part by the term "easy-believism."

The most common form of easy-believism is say-a-prayer-and-you-are-saved, often combined with walking down the church aisle. Critics call this decisional regeneration, fire insurance from hell, easy-believism, or accepting Christ as your Savior and not as your Lord. These techniques "work" because many Evangelicals want the cheap grace and discounted duties of a populist gospel.¹ Indeed, it is a cultural gospel fashioned for a democracy of equality of conditions and individualism. Bourgeois Christians like the free-grace gospel because they understand free to mean no obligation to God; but the Bible does not teach that the people of God have no duty to their God.

Easy-believism simplifies salvation by making faith a matter of having correct biblical thoughts about you as sinner and Jesus as Savior and his sacrifice on the cross. Having these correct thoughts in your mind and "accepting" them saves you. Consequently, "leading someone to Christ" is often an intellectual event, not a spiritual rebirth. Having the theologically correct thoughts in your mind is supposedly manifested in the words of the prayer for salvation often called the Sinner's Prayer.

In its essence, decisional regeneration calls for an intellectual assent to a few biblical ideas. This is often the first step toward the intellectualized Christianity that many Evangelicals live.² And as sociologist George Ritzer explains, "The cultural products of postmodern society do not delve deeply into underlying meanings."³ Or, as philosopher Karl Jaspers says: "One of the most notable characteristics of our day is a progressive and irremediable loss of substance."⁴ Shallow meanings make shallow Christians, and our culture thrives on shallow meanings. The populism that controls much evangelical religion produces weak Christians, if it produces Christians at all.

But more importantly, the thin theology of American revivalism disenchants the gospel by making "accepting Christ as your Savior" a mechanical act of saying a prayer after accepting some biblical concepts in your mind. Mechanizing the gospel, however, takes the power and mystery out of it and thereby disenchants it. It makes salvation a mind event, not a life-altering transformation. And easy-believism incites another problem—consumerism.

---

1. Once again, this is part of the modern age. As Søren Kierkegaard explained in 1843: "Not only in the commercial world but in the realm of ideas as well, our age is holding a veritable clearance sale. Everything is had so dirt cheap that it is doubtful whether in the end there is anyone who will bid" (*Fear and Trembling*, 3).

2. Dr. Martyn Lloyd-Jones describes the difference in faith and intellectual assent: the one with faith is the one who does the will of the Father. "The difference between faith and intellectual assent is that intellectual assent simply says, 'Lord, Lord', but does not do His will. In other words, though I may say 'Lord, Lord' to the Lord Jesus Christ, there is no meaning in it unless I regard Him as my Lord, and willingly become His bondslave" (*First Book of Daily Readings*, 65).

3. Ritzer, *McDonaldization of Society*, 48.

4. Jaspers, *Man in the Modern Age*, 86.

Consumerism is the desire to have more, buy more, and spend more for personal pleasure and fulfillment. It focuses on the self, and a gratified self is the goal. In fact, consumerism is one of the dominant characteristics of American culture. Consumer capitalism drives our economy, and advertising drives the buyer. These join to instill a consumerist outlook and a please-me ethic that seeks what gratifies at the best price and the least time spent.

Unfortunately, this consumerist mentality has waded into the churches and made many Evangelicals religious consumers. They take what pleases them, but they don't give back. They look for churches with good music and good preaching—the aesthetic—and they sit, but they don't serve. In other words, they don't stop being consumers when they come to church. But it is not just consumerism. It is the aesthete's approach to the Christian life that rests in what pleases but avoids commitment. And as Jean-Jacques Rousseau explained centuries ago: "Once a man has grown accustomed to prefer his life to his duty, he will soon also prefer to it the things that make life easy and agreeable."[5] The easy and agreeable appeals to the aesthetic self. So what is the aesthetic self?

We live in the age of aestheticism, and philosopher Luc Ferry says that modern man is *homo aestheticus*.[6] Likewise, Alasdair MacIntyre observes that the aesthete is one of the central characters of the modern age or one of the dominant models for how to live a fulfilling life.[7] In the modern age, the aesthetic has replaced the ethical in churches because Bourgeois Christian aesthetes take a sensible and reflective approach to the Christian life and lack passion. On occasion they may flare up into short-lived enthusiasm, but they soon relax back into a prudential indolence. That is how Kierkegaard described the Bourgeois Christians of his era.[8] And it still defines today's evangelical aesthetes, the Bourgeois Christians.

Evangelical aesthetes consume religious goods produced by a comfortable and populist Christianity with its blue-jean casualness. But the aesthete's focus is not so much on pleasure as it is on finding what is

---

5. Rousseau, *Discourses*, 57.
6. Ferry, *Homo Aestheticus*, 7–22.
7. MacIntyre, *After Virtue*, 228.
8. Kierkegaard, *Two Ages*, 68. "The present age is essentially a *sensible, reflecting age, devoid of passion, flaring up in superficial, short-lived enthusiasm and prudentially relaxing in indolence.*" Emphasis in original.

interesting that brings pleasure.⁹ Accordingly, good sermons, biblical insights, and the signs of the apocalypse are interesting and keep the aesthetes coming back to church. Aesthetes enjoy entertainment, and one of the hallmarks of a church with aesthetic-focused members is good preaching. The Christian aesthetes want good preaching because it pleases them, but it doesn't change them. They become connoisseurs of sermons and critics of preachers. But they hear the sermon aesthetically, not existentially and ethically, and the aesthetic rarely changes lives; it only changes minds and usually just briefly. This is moralistic therapeutic theism.¹⁰ They believe in the God of the Bible. They live moral lives, and it is therapeutic because it makes them feel good and releases them from working in God's kingdom. It also makes them critics.

For example, the pastor of a large church left his pulpit to preach in an inner-city church. One of his members followed him and heard him preach. Afterwards she commented on how relaxed he was in the pulpit. He explained that he was relaxed because he was not preaching to his usual critical audience. A critical audience is an aesthete audience. The fundamental failure of aesthete Christians in this context is that they enjoy the sermon, feel good about themselves because they hear it, and then forget it. But the opposite of the aesthetic is the earnest, and "earnestness is to will to listen in order to will to do accordingly."¹¹ But there is more: along with aesthetic consumerism, we find a related cultural force at work in the churches—populism.

The easy-believism gospel is a kind of religious populism. Populism is the scheme or plan that gives the people what they want, whether it is good for them or not, or whether it is true or not. It is pandering to their desires. It

---

9. Paul David Tripp gives a good example of this aesthetic understanding: "Faith is something that you do with your life. True biblical faith doesn't stop with thought; it radically rearranges the way that you approach everything in your life. Amazement [an aesthetic response] is what you experience when you are taken beyond the categories that you carry around to explain or define things. Amazement is a step in the faith process, but there is a huge difference between amazement and faith" (*New Morning Mercies*, June 27). For example, finding Jesus hidden in the Old Testament may be amazing and, therefore, interesting to the aesthete, but it must lead to the ethical/existential, not hide it.

10. The term "moralistic therapeutic deism" was coined by Christian Smith in 2005 (Smith with Denton, *Soul Searching*). Smith's book reports on the religious and spiritual lives of American teenagers. Many of these teenagers have a deistic view of God like the deism of eighteenth-century Europe. By contrast, Bourgeois Christians have a theistic viewpoint consistent with a biblical view of God.

11. Kierkegaard, *Upbuilding Discourses*, 123.

is a political concept that I apply to religion. Populism dilutes to the average, the emotional, and the ordinary; it thins the truth and hides the duty. A flood tide of populism has washed away the salt and the sting of the gospel.

Populism comes in various strains: one strain is revivalism, and another strain is a skinny intellectualism. One is lowbrow; the other is highbrow, but narrowly focused. And as Professor Wells explains so concisely: "At this very moment, evangelicalism has bought cultural acceptability by emptying itself of serious thought, serious theology, serious worship, and serious practice in the larger culture."[12] Evangelical populism is a sellout to the culture. It is worldly. I call it populism because it is what many Evangelicals want.

In a populist Christianity, the "aesthetic" or consumer Christians enjoy good food, good wines, good books, and good church, all with a casual style. And the populist gospel of easy-believism says because you repeated the right words, now you are going to heaven when you die. It empties the gospel of serious thought and the Christian life of serious action. The decision becomes the focus of the "believer's" salvation. They don't recognize it, but they have turned the prayer into the one work that saves them.

The Bible teaches that works don't save, and most Evangelicals will tell you that. But they don't understand that easy-believism teaches that there is one work that will save you—saying the Sinner's Prayer. Because when they say, "I said the Sinner's Prayer, so I'm saved," they have turned the gospel prayer into a work. This is typical decisional regeneration, and by pandering to the individualistic, democratic culture, many Evangelicals have sold out the deeper things of God. Indeed, populism in this context means giving the people the gospel they want or giving them the god they want. Populism also transforms God's kingdom into "my kingdom come; my will be done." And because I said the prayer, now God is happy with me.

In fact, the easy-believism crowd is like the Judeans of Jeremiah's time. They too had a cultural religion, just like many Evangelicals. And J. Gresham Machen describes them well: "The people of Jerusalem at the time of Jeremiah had no doubt; they were quite sure that God was for them; but they went into exile all the same; God was not for them at all."[13] And easy-believism populism has the same effect. It instills a false confidence about the prayer-sayer's relationship with God.

---

12. Wells, *God in the Wasteland*, 27.
13. Machen, *What Is Faith?*, 79.

Christian populism is not new. Alexis de Tocqueville noted in America in the 1830s that "religion itself reigns there far less as revealed doctrine than as common opinion."[14] The easy-believism gospel is populism applied to the gospel. It is the common-opinion gospel. It is pragmatic in the sense that it works in a worldly way. But the cheap and easy gospel of populist individualism dumbs down the Christian life and Christian truth, and as philosopher Karl Jaspers notes, "Empirical observation supports the truth of the proposition which obtrudes itself on us time and again, that the greater the number of people who understand something, the less substance it has."[15] The pop gospel has little substance. Tocqueville calls this shallowness "general ideas," and revivalist ideas about the gospel are shallow and adopted for convenience, but not for conviction. This is the new orthodoxy, the democratic, populist orthodoxy of many Evangelicals.

And so goes the American revivalism version of the gospel—widely understood but with little salt. In many evangelical circles, the mystery of the gospel has become so easy to understand that it means little, and this reflects worldliness—the universal leveling spirit of the age.[16] Leveling comes with individualism, populism, and a democratic culture. Indeed, they require it. Leveling the gospel disenchants the word of God by mechanizing salvation through a prayer. And when the mystery is gone, much of the power goes with it. The disenchanted gospel is the gospel the people want. This is leveling down the Christian life for anyone who will say the prayer.

Professor Wells describes the leveling spirit in this way: "The constant cultural bombardment of individualism, in the absence of a robust theology, meant that faith that had rightly been understood as personal now easily became faith that was individualistic, self-focused, and consumer oriented."[17] The populist gospel is a kind of herd Christianity, and for Kierkegaard, herd Christianity is retaining the metaphysics of the faith while repudiating its morality.[18] In other words, herd Christians in intellectualist churches embrace the theology but neglect the neighbor. This levels the Christian life and Christian truth. Of course, you can always dumb down

---

14. Tocqueville, *Democracy in America*, 492. Interestingly and presciently, Tocqueville predicts that faith in public opinion will become a sort of religion with the majority as a sort of prophet.

15. Jaspers, *Basic Philosophical Writings*, 76.

16. Tocqueville, *Democracy in America*, 5.

17. Wells, *Courage to Be Protestant*, 11.

18. Westphal, "Kierkegaard's Sociology," 134.

Christianity to a low bar that everyone can meet and then claim success for your ministry. Indeed, as one Presbyterian minister admitted, we have made Christianity "cheap" to grow our churches.[19]

Contrary to what Wells argues, someone can have robust theology and still desert the neighbor morality of Christian duty. This follows from the knowledge-culture mentality that valorizes theology, doctrine, and learning. This is a highbrow kind of leveling. It anthropomorphizes God and turns him into a theologian. Doctrine puts thought in the foreground and action in the background. Someone can swim well in an ocean of robust theology only to drown in the narrow channels of intellectualism. Indeed, Wells's classical Evangelicals are often well anchored in the faith, but anchored ships don't sail. Being a Christian is much more than having thoughts about being a Christian. Life is a series of personal situations, not a series of psychological events. The aesthetic is important, but it can't stand alone. The beauty of Christ is important, but the example of the servant Christ is largely forgotten.

Paradoxically, while the knowledge culture's urging for more theological robustness and the revivalist culture's populist gospel seem at odds, in fact, they converge in believing that what is in the mind is what counts. For example, well-known Evangelical John R. W. Stott says that "how we think determines how we act," but he is wrong.[20] What we *will* determines how we act.

It helps to remember the parable of the two sons (Matt 21:28–31). The father went to his two sons and told them to go work in the vineyard. The first son told his father he would not go, but then relented and went to work. The second son said he would go but did not. The second son had the right thoughts, but no action followed from those thoughts. And as Jesus says, the one who worked did his father's will. Many good thoughts end in no action because of a failure of will. But Stott's statement demonstrates a popular and crippling intellectualist's focus on right thinking.

I suspect that Stott thinks he is quoting Prov 23:7, but he is not. Rather, the KJV says this: "For as he thinketh in his *heart*, so is he" (emphasis added). But when you leave heart out of the verse, you have cut out the central point. (See ch. 8, "The Centrality of the Heart.") In fact, twelve verses later, Prov 23:19 describes the biblical order: "Listen, my son, and be wise

---

19. Farnsworth, "Is It Too Much."
20. Stott, *Ephesians*, 43.

[correct thoughts], and direct your heart in the way [action]." The Bible inexorably connects thought to will and will to action.

Many Evangelicals, however, have no idea that the vast sponge of the world system has sucked them in, and that the crowd, the herd, populism, and consumerism control their thinking. They don't look in the mirror and see their aesthetic selves. Consequently, they follow the populist god and live an average Christian life, and this is usually true no matter how many times a week they go to church or how robust their theology is. Dumbing down the Christian life ends in distracting and misdirecting believers, and self-seeking, not serving, characterizes the age.

In this populist understanding, biblical truth gets transformed into worldly wisdom or populist clichés using biblical words. I call this biblespeak or godtalk.[21] This is a paradox. Bible words sink in a quicksand of cultural meanings. The paradox is complicated because thin theology becomes authoritative. It supplants the density of biblical truth and the mystery of God's redemptive plan. Thin theology deconstructs the Bible's central truth to a few "laws."

Few recognize the paradox that these easy-believism salvation rituals help create Bourgeois Christians. They cannot see that this kind of evangelism inoculates people against the gospel, nor do they see the poverty of action that it justifies. And here is how this thin theology works: Joe tells me, "John became a Christian last night." I ask, "How do you know?" Joe says, "I know he is saved because he said the Sinner's Prayer, so he is saved. And once saved, always saved." For revivalism, salvation is an event, not a process, and that makes the prayer an incantation.

Another example: The church leader's wife describes her friend and says that "she is saved because she accepted Christ as her Savior, even though she is living like the devil now. At least she has her fire insurance." And a final example, which confuses the demonic for the sacred, is the "Christian" who spent his life molesting children, but he is in heaven today "because he believed, and that's what matters." Many Evangelicals believe in decisional salvation because that is what they have been taught by well-known evangelists. They also have been taught this unwittingly through the knowledge culture's emphasis that right knowledge saves, and right knowledge pleases God. But the paradoxes of revivalism go deeper.

---

21. The way I use the word "biblespeak" reminds me of a quote by Dorothy Sayers: "I always have a quotation for everything—it saves original thinking." This sounds like Tocqueville's notion of general ideas being the way Americans think.

This consumerist, populist, average kind of Christianity follows the moral relativism of the age with its own Christian relativism, not so much in thought, but in action. Thinking the right things about biblical truth justifies failing to do works of love. This is evangelical Gnosticism. It is a mind/body dualism: the mind matters; the body doesn't. Many Evangelicals who scorn moral relativism live a biblical relativism supported by the easy-believism gospel.

As noted above, easy-believism turns salvation into an intellectual transaction, not a spiritual transformation. From the beginning it teaches about the me-ness of your faith—God's wonderful plan for *you*, and for *you* to get saved, *you* have to say a prayer and that is all *you* do; and then *you* get to say, "I [*you*] found it," when, in fact, God found you. It panders to the individualism of the age. "You did it, and that finishes it" is very comforting.

I have been describing the paradoxes of certain evangelism techniques and how many Evangelicals fail to see the harm these techniques create. I am not saying this occurs every time someone evangelizes or every time someone prays for God's forgiveness. I am simply saying that it happens and that how the pop gospel misdirects Evangelicals is hidden. Moreover, I'm not saying that this type of evangelism is the problem. It is just part of the problem—just one more dying star in the constellation of the evangelical knowledge culture bound up in a populist and consumerist gospel that swallows spirituality into a black hole. The list of problems that easy-believism creates goes on.

Easy-believism teaches that salvation means enjoying God's wonderful plan for your life now and going to heaven when you die. It does not teach, and indeed avoids teaching that God recruits Christians to block and tackle in the kingdom of God, which is why Christians need the full armor of God. It teaches that God's kingdom is in heaven, not on earth. But a blocking and tackling Christianity does not fit well with the comfortable aesthetic Christianity that prevails in many evangelical churches.

Further, as part of the populist gospel, Bourgeois Christians want to complicate the simple and simplify the complex. For example, according to the Bible, salvation is complicated: foreknowledge, predestination, calling, justification, adoption, sanctification, glorification—all a part of the mystery of Christ.[22] But Bourgeois Christians simplify it into a prayer. On

---

22. The theological terms listed here are discrete actions of redemption described in the Bible. *Justification* is God's act in declaring a sinner righteous based on the imputed work of Christ. *Sanctification* is a process empowered by God over a believer's lifetime to overcome the power and dominion of sin. Both justification and sanctification arise

the other hand, "faith without works is dead" is a simple biblical truth, but they complicate it by calling it a mystery, by not talking about it at all, or by saying that it comes from the book of James that Luther calls the epistle of straw. No wonder American Evangelicals have little clout with the culture. They are too much a part of it. And as Phillip Rieff says, "Nowadays, the world is full of tame Christians; in consequence, the churches are empty of life, if not of people."[23]

So why are Christians tame? This raises another problem with contemporary Christianity—privatization. Privatization tames the Christian religion by making it personal and private. Os Guinness calls it the private-zoo factor.[24] It is, in part, one outcome of an individualistic culture. It is what the world system allows Christians after four hundred years of secularization. A privatized religion is limited to your personal life and not allowed in the public square. It may be privately important, but it is socially irrelevant. One example is the Christian businessman who never misses Sunday church but whose business practices are pagan. Christian values become weekend values or home values. The light may shine on the weekend, but it goes out during the week. As Guinness explains, "If we can ensure that faith is *personal but no more*, then we can quietly coax it into a corner from which it will never emerge."[25]

Bourgeois Christianity is a cultural religion, not a biblical religion. Bourgeois Christians' faith is in Bourgeois Christianity, not a biblical Christianity. They drift in the tides of culture, but they don't recognize how the pagan flood controls them. Novelist David Foster Wallace tells a story about not recognizing the familiar:

> There are these two young fish swimming along and they happen to meet an older fish swimming the other way, who nods at them and says "Morning, boys. How's the water?" And the two young fish swim on for a bit, and then eventually one of them looks over at the other and goes "What the hell is water?"[26]

They were unaware of the obvious just like so many Evangelicals trapped in the culture who don't understand their worldliness.

from the work of Christ.

23. Rieff, *Triumph of the Therapeutic*, 84.

24. Guinness, *Gravedigger File*, 73–74. Many of the ideas on privatization come from this very helpful book.

25. Guinness, *Gravedigger File*, 75. Emphasis in original.

26. Wallace, "This Is Water," para. 1.

I conclude part 1 with this thought: The history of the West for the past one hundred years shows an ever-diminishing role for human responsibility. Abortion, no-fault divorce, and decriminalizing drug abuse are just a few examples of this decline. The beyond-good-and-evil society bears the cost of the loss of human responsibility that brings with it the loss of human dignity. This is the way of the world, and as I have shown in part 1, many Evangelicals have followed the spirit of the age by shirking their responsibility to their God. Next, part 2 describes the evangelical knowledge culture and its counter-Christian influence on the biblical call to action.

Part II: Descartes, the Cartesian Consciousness, and the Evangelical Knowledge Culture

Chapter 5 The Intellectualist Way of Being a Christian

BOURGEOIS CHRISTIANS LIVE IN a church knowledge culture. In a knowledge culture, what you know is what matters. A Christian knowledge culture stresses knowing God's word, teaching doctrine, and preaching exegetically. It is a teaching-learning culture. What could be wrong with that? But the Bourgeois Christian knowledge culture sends the message that what counts in the Christian life is what you know about the Bible. Certainly, what believers know is important, but what believers do with what they know matters much more. Jesus calls his disciples to bear fruit and do good works, but a knowing-but-not-doing spirituality is sterile. This sterile spirituality is the disengaged Christian life of the Bourgeois Christian, not the incarnate and embodied life of presenting "your bodies a living and holy sacrifice, . . . which is your spiritual service of worship" (Rom 12:1). It is not a lifetime of doing "good works, which God prepared beforehand so that we would walk in them" (Eph 2:10).

In fact, serving characterizes Christianity because God set up his kingdom as a kingdom of service and calls his children to serve in that kingdom. Ephesians 2:10 says: "For we are God's workmanship, created in Christ Jesus to do good works, which God prepared in advance for us to do" (NIV). This is fundamental. The apostle Paul exhorts in Rom 12:1: "Offer your bodies as living sacrifices" (NIV). Indeed, good works show God's power in believers' lives—that they truly believe, love, and serve God (Jas 2:17, 24).[1] Paradoxically, the Christian knowledge culture works against

---

1. "To affect any knowledge of God that is not to be itself known and ascertained by the keeping of his commandments—to dream of knowing God otherwise than in the

God's service kingdom, which is God's ethical pattern for life. This knowledge focus is the Cartesian consciousness of Bourgeois Christianity, and at its heart lies a deep worldliness. But this is not new. As Dutch Calvinist Herman Ridderbos explains, Judaism "had divorced the law from the living God, and had made the law merely a subject for formal and scholarly learning."[2] The old knowledge culture has transformed into the new knowledge culture of Bourgeois Christianity.

We can understand the evangelical knowledge culture by another name: Christian intellectualism.[3] In an intellectualist Christianity, Bible knowledge becomes an end in itself, not a tool to serve God. Christian duty becomes learning, understanding, and organizing biblical truth. Learning is the way to please God and get closer to him.

Moreover, in a knowledge culture, believers must understand the theological system and get the right doctrinal picture in their minds. The intellect, the believer's consciousness, becomes the focus of the intellectualized Christian life, and this is rooted in ancient Greek thought and the pagan tradition that follows it. For example, the Neoplatonist Plotinus says: "And intellectual activity is ours in the sense that the soul is intellectual and intellectual activity is its higher life, both when the soul operates intellectually and when intellect acts upon us. For intellect too is a part of ourselves and to it we ascend." Or, he puts it more poetically: "But how do we possess God? He rides mounted on the nature of Intellect and true reality—that is how we possess him."[4]

For Plotinus, the higher spirituality comes from using the intellect, which he calls the soul of religion, and Neoplatonist piety models itself on the activity of the intellect. It gathers and synthesizes religious truth for the mind.[5] The Neoplatonists are forebearers of Bourgeois Christian intellectualism. Indeed, Classics Professor R. T. Wallis explains that "the dominant trend of Christian theology . . . has always been Neoplatonic."[6] The Neoplatonists influenced Augustine, and Augustine influenced Calvin. For

---

way of keeping his commandments—is to be false to the heart's core" (Candlish, *Commentary on 1 John*, 80).

2. Ridderbos, *Coming of the Kingdom*, 314.

3. This narrow kind of intellectualism, a denominational intellectualism, is completely consistent with the anti-intellectualism that Mark Noll describes in *The Scandal of the Evangelical Mind*. My use of this term is complex and unfolds in this chapter and others.

4. Plotinus, *Porphyry on Plotinus*, 111.

5. Levinas, *Alterity and Transcendence*, 10–11.

6. Wallis, *Neoplatonism*, 160.

example, Calvinist theologian Charles Hodge describes "a much higher kind of knowledge" that comes from systematic theology.[7] Calvinist J. Gresham Machen, the founder of Westminster Theological Seminary, defends "the primacy of the intellect."[8] This does not mean, however, that Bourgeois Christians are intellectuals as we commonly use that term. In fact, this narrow intellectualism is just one model for being a Christian.

The intellectualist model, however, is not based on how much education you have or how intellectual you are. Indeed, it is anti-intellectual, which is one of the reasons Evangelicals can't identify pagan thought and practice in their midst. When the knowledge culture prevails over an ethical culture in a church, Evangelicals know the Bible but do little for God's kingdom. For example, Bourgeois Christian dispensationalists understand the intricacies of the rapture and the apocalypse, and Bourgeois Christian Presbyterians understand the complexities of the Reformed Faith, but they both neglect the Christian neighbor ethic of sacrifice for others. This is Christian intellectualism, and too much emphasis on biblical knowledge paradoxically fosters an unfruitful Christianity.

Furthermore, intellectualism cultivates theological correctness, not neighborly beneficence, and it induces spiritual torpor, not spiritual vigor. Knowledge drifts around in the mind, but the biblical model for being a Christian means walking with the feet, working with the hands, and serving with the heart while being embedded in a community.

The intellectualist model falls short because the knowledge culture of Bourgeois Christianity leads the heart away from serving and directs it to learning. This kind of intellectualism offers an escape from an existential Christianity through an aesthetic release. A what-I-need-to-know Christianity replaces a what-I-need-to-do Christianity that contradicts Jesus's warning that "whoever believes in me will also do the works that I do" (John 14:12).

For example, this intellectualism produces clericalism, a spiritual condition often found in many evangelical churches where the church members leave the church work to the paid church staff.[9] Dithering with duty

---

7. Hodge, *Systematic Theology*, 1:2.

8. Machen, *What Is Faith?*, 26.

9. An unpublished "Church Health Survey" prepared by the Lawless Group for First Presbyterian Church, Macon, Sept. 2007. One of the unhealthy categories was: "Most of the ministry in our church is done by a small number of people." Lawless states: "1.65 is your church's average score for this question, from a maximum score of 4.00. This is a LOW response compared to the others in this particular church function. The

characterizes the intellectualist model. But as Pascal understood centuries ago, the knowledge of God is very far from the love of him.[10]

Knowledge not tied to action and quickened by emotion becomes barren and dry. It yields orthodoxy but not right conduct and right emotions. This biblical intellectualism thrives in Reformed, dispensationalist, and fundamentalist churches. Twentieth-century Spanish philosopher Miguel de Unamuno concisely defines the problem of Christian intellectualism as "seeking to believe with the reason and not with life."[11] But this kind of intellectualism is typical of the modern-age focus on the mind, and as Martin Heidegger explains, "Modern thought grasps all beings in terms of consciousness."[12]

Although I call evangelical intellectualism and its focus on consciousness a spiritual problem, we can understand it better if we analyze it as an ethical failure. Ethical systems set standards for behavior, prescribe right and prohibit wrong conduct, set goals, and define the moral principles that underlie the system. Ethical systems describe how one should live. Importantly, ethics order a community and demand action within that community.

At the heart of the Christian religion lies the ethical question of how to live the Christian life in a community. What does it mean to live as a Christian in twenty-first-century America? We can simplify the question by asking whether the intellectualist model of Bourgeois Christianity or the Eph 2:10 embodied-service model better represents Christian living.

The intellectualist model holds sway in a subset of American Evangelicals who consider themselves "true believers" because of their orthodoxy and not because of their actions. Orthodoxy is their action. The intellectualist model describes the essence and aim of Christian living and the mode of being a Christian for many Evangelicals who attend Bible-believing churches.

A model for being a Christian describes the pattern of how believers live the Christian life, the path they walk, and their goals. Pentecostalism and Pietism are models for the Christian life, as are the intellectualist model and the embodied-service model.[13] The emphases, interests, focus, and

---

membership sees the bulk of ministry done by a few in the church."

10. Pascal, *Pensées*, 92.

11. Unamuno, *Tragic Sense of Life*, 49. He is referring to the Catholic Church.

12. Heidegger, *Holderlin's Hymn "The Ister,"* 94.

13. Much contemporary Pentecostalism is characterized by emotionalism and a

action or lack thereof determine the model. But these models or patterns are not precise; they are general.

Not every Evangelical follows one model or another, and even in intellectualist churches and denominations, one can find embodied-service model Christians who work hard in the kingdom of God. In other words, not every Evangelical is a Bourgeois Christian, and some Evangelicals are more bourgeois than others. Indeed, many Evangelicals serve God daily and do not fit the Bourgeois Christian definition or sink into gnostic intellectualism.

Consequently, the intellectualist model and the embodied-service model are not fixed positions but rather represent a continuum and an emphasis. The more service characterizes the believer's life, the more the Eph 2:10 embodied model prevails. These models, however, turn on the ethical question: What does it mean to be a Christian? Or to ask the question in a different way: What does the Christian life require?

Unfortunately, the Bourgeois Christian problem is more complex than it first appears. It involves more than a choice between models of the Christian life and the relationship between knowledge and service. For example, it not only goes to the heart of what it means to be a Christian but also asks what biblical truth is. Many Evangelicals do not understand what truth is, and the truth problem influences the being-a-Christian question.

Evangelicals have a wrong view of truth because they have an incomplete view of it, and in their worldliness, they adopt the culture's understanding of truth. This worldly Cartesian consciousness promotes a half-truth or lazy-truth Christianity. The chapter titled "The Truth Is *Aletheia*" deals with this problem. How believers understand truth and how they live it are central to the Christian life, and truth is not something merely held in consciousness.

The Cartesian consciousness drives Bourgeois Christianity when it sends the message that what you know about truth is what counts; therefore, strive to know more. No doubt many Evangelicals will object that their church does not teach that "knowing is what counts," and I do not dispute that. But in no way does that diminish my argument, because even if that is

---

focus on the individual receiving the Holy Spirit. Pietism manifests itself as a religion of individual practices emphasizing attending church functions, regular prayer, having quiet times, tithing, reading Christian literature, and living a moral life. These models tend to be self-reflecting, self-centered, and individualistic, and thus contrary to loving one's neighbor. Moreover, the "moral life" tends to be a life of pagan virtue masquerading as Christian virtue. Pentecostalism and Pietism can both lead to a privatized religion.

not taught directly, it is taught indirectly. If preachers preach doctrinal sermons, and if Sunday School teachers teach biblical lessons, and if churches offer scripture-based discipleship programs, why does clericalism prevail in so many churches? How does this lifeless and heartless Christianity originate even in the churches with pastors who preach the Reformed faith? Why do they produce the frozen chosen? Herein lies the subtlety of the worldliness of the Bourgeois Christian knowledge problem and the dark clouds of paradoxes that hide Christian truth while teaching it. In fact, and paradoxically, biblical sermons can obscure biblical truth. What is intended as light dims truth. This happens without church leaders recognizing it.

The intellectualist emphasis arises from the structures of the church. These structures include the emphases of programs, the pastor's preaching, and the denomination's traditions. For example, in churches with the intellectualist influence, the worship service focuses on preaching, and the church staff devises programs to help members learn more. Teaching the lesson dominates the Sunday School hour, and pastors push members to join Bible studies or journey groups to learn more about the Bible.[14] Officer training focuses on doctrine, and children learn the catechism. But here is the paradox: all this training is valuable until it creates the message that what you know about the Bible is what really counts, not serving your neighbor.

The intellectualist emphasis also arises from our culture. In *Philosophical Investigations*, one of the most important books of twentieth-century philosophy, Ludwig Wittgenstein describes the effect that speech has on us:

> That is to say, we are so much accustomed to communicating in speech, in conversation, that it looks to us as if the whole point of communicating lay in this: that someone else grasps the sense of my words—which is something mental—that he, as it were, takes it into his own mind. If he then does something further with it as well, that is no part of the immediate purpose of language.[15]

The goal of speech becomes communicating ideas in a way that hearers can grasp them. Hearers come to understand that this is their job, their foremost job, in our do-you-get-it culture and not the biblical do-you-do-it culture. Characteristic of evangelical intellectualism, communication,

---

14. As one prominent PCA leader explains about small groups: "Everything the church does is based on God's Word, so the most important thing is to provide sound biblical instruction" (Ryken, *City on a Hill*, 89).

15. Wittgenstein, *Philosophical Investigations*, 121.

not action, is foremost. And although pastors will quickly say that this is not what they intend, they must overcome the communication culture to defeat the passive piety that comes with it. But the problem goes deeper into worldliness.

Christian truth is often presented as a picture, but the age of the world-picture, our age, promotes a pagan understanding of truth.[16] Martin Heidegger calls truth as picture the fundamental event of the modern age.[17] The picture becomes something to grasp with the intellect. He further says that Christendom turns Christian doctrine into a worldview.[18] Consequently, in the age of world-picture, the goal becomes right understanding. The problem is that someone can have a Christian world-picture that is not biblical.

In the world-picture of the evangelical knowledge culture, something gets twisted backwards. Believers read a sacred text, a Christian book, or listen to a sermon as an object to understand. This is backwards because the learner is the object of Christian truth; truth is not the object. The learner is the object of the truth because truth should transform, not just enlighten. Orthodoxy is not the goal; action is.

Furthermore, many evangelical preachers assume that orthodoxy produces right action; but orthodoxy involves the mind, while action combines the mind, the will, and the body. Even worse, for Bourgeois Christians orthodoxy replaces action. But as Paul David Tripp explains, "Faith surely does engage your brain, but it is fundamentally more than that. Faith is something that you do with your life. True biblical faith doesn't stop with thought; it radically rearranges the way that you approach everything in your life."[19] This is the ethical system that the intellectualist influence obstructs.

As a result, church structures can convey a self-defeating message even when the preacher never proclaims it. For example, the well-intended "get in the word," when urged in intellectualist churches, can convey that learning and knowing really count, so the learners and knowers increase their knowledge while neglecting kingdom work. ("Get in the neighborhood" works better.) When the preacher's main task is teaching the Bible, the congregation senses that their main task is to learn it. Hence, they become Christian

---

16. See generally Heidegger, *Question Concerning Technology*, 115–54.
17. Heidegger, *Question Concerning Technology*, 134.
18. Heidegger, *Question Concerning Technology*, 117.
19. Tripp, *New Morning Mercies*, June 27.

learners and not Christian doers, and they become victims of unintended consequences. Paradoxically, the wrong emphasis can defeat the call to Christian duty, and "get in the word" becomes a shibboleth, a password to avoid doing kingdom work—another paradox.

More importantly, the cause of this evangelical intellectualism and the spiritual poverty that flows from it is iatrogenic. Although that term seems out of place, it fits the spiritual malady of intellectualism because *iatrogenic* describes an injury or illness that your doctor inflicts on you. In other words, pastors, teachers, and theologians have unwittingly promoted the Cartesian consciousness. By deciding that teaching the word is their main task and that the congregation's main task is to learn the word, they confirm the intellectualist message and set the wrong goals. The controlling idea is no longer love; it is knowledge. This is true whether they realize it or not. On the other hand, if they had the goal of making servants of God, they would take a different approach, although preaching, teaching, and sound doctrine would still be important. An analogy will help here.

The Continental Divide begins in Montana and runs south along the Rocky Mountains and into New Mexico. This line of mountains has a critical hydrological effect because it forms two separate watersheds. Rain and snow that fall on the west side of the Continental Divide drain into the Pacific Ocean. Rain and snow that fall on the east side of the divide drain into the Atlantic Ocean. Hence, the starting position of the water determines where it flows.

In a similar way, if preachers understand that they are called to preach the word and make sure that their flocks think correct biblical thoughts, they will minister in one way. But if they strive to make servants of God, to have their congregations love their neighbors, and to humble themselves and be servants as Christ was a servant, they will follow a different approach. No doubt, teaching and preaching will be important, but from this different emphasis, a different structure and a different focus will follow.

Evangelicals may have difficulty grasping the hidden-message concept and its effect in their church, but it is easy to see how a denomination's teaching influences how its followers live the Christian life and how it shapes their goals. For example, the Pentecostals take their name and their pursuit of spirituality from Acts 2. The Holy Spirit came with a violent wind and tongues of fire, and believers began to speak in tongues. Many Pentecostals focus on getting "the second blessing" from the Holy Spirit and having the Holy Spirit's power for speaking in tongues and healing. And while Bourgeois Christians seek more knowledge, many

Pentecostals seek the baptism of the Holy Spirit, and the holy water comes down one side of the mountains for the Pentecostals and the other side of the mountains for the intellectualist denominations.

Another example may help. Professor Karen Dieleman of Trinity Christian College has written a helpful book entitled *Religious Imaginaries: The Liturgical and Poetic Practices of Elizabeth Barrett Browning, Christina Rossetti, and Adelaide Proctor*. In this book she shows how the liturgies in these women's churches influenced their poetry. As Dieleman explains: "Sustained practices—of any kind—have a powerful formative effect on how we imagine the world and our place in it and consequently on how we talk or write about it."[20] Church tradition and practices influence how their members understand what it means to be a Christian.

In churches, where you start and what you esteem influence your goals for the Christian life. Browning's churches emphasized preaching the word; Rossetti's emphasized the sacraments and community. The poets were given models or paradigms of Christian piety. They were shown the "real" Christianity and how to pursue the Christian life. Their different views about spirituality affected how they wrote their poetry. Dieleman shows that church structures can encourage or discourage models or types of spirituality, even when the pastors and the members of the congregations do not recognize it.

But these models are denominational even when much of what they include is biblical. For example, the knowledge paradigm is biblical in many ways. The problem arises when the knowledge paradigm trumps the service paradigm of the ethical system. If you build a knowledge overemphasis into your church, you will produce many learners and few doers. This kind of Christian intellectualism, this focus on orthodoxy, too often begins and ends in orthodoxy.

In the next chapter, I explain what the Cartesian consciousness is and how it promotes the disembodied life of Bourgeois Christianity that characterizes so much of American Evangelicalism. Indeed, "so much of the history of epistemology is one of different attempts to *disembody* the knower or to hide his or her embodiment."[21] The age pushes people to disembodied thinking. This is a new version of the old Gnosticism. It induces a mind/body dualism that is both anti-biblical and difficult to detect because it is so deeply embedded in Western thinking.

---

20. Dieleman, *Religious Imaginaries*, 6.
21. Ihde, *Bodies in Technology*, 68. Emphasis in original.

Chapter 6 The Cartesian Elements of the Cartesian Consciousness

THE CARTESIAN CONSCIOUSNESS OF Bourgeois Christianity is worldly. This chapter addresses why, what effect this worldliness has, and how it leads to a Christian spirituality disengaged from American culture. More specifically, this chapter identifies the worldly origin of disengagement and how it begets clericalism. Also, I explain why I chose "Cartesian" to describe this state of consciousness.

Describing the Cartesian consciousness begins with Rene Descartes's *cogito, ergo sum*—I think, therefore I am. Descartes's ideas still influence how we live in the twenty-first century, and it can be difficult for someone not trained in philosophy to understand Descartes's profound influence. Professor Michael Allen Gillespie describes it well: "*Ego cogito ergo sum* is engraved over one of the great gateways to modernity, and we who have passed through this gateway have come under its spell. Indeed we have been transformed by it, for this principle has helped give a new meaning to what it is to be a human being and thus helps establish a whole new range of political, ethical, and philosophical possibilities."[1] It has also transformed religious understanding. In many ways we live in a Cartesian culture because we live in a scientific age. But the Cartesian perspective produces not only the scientific viewpoint; it has colonized common sense, common talk, and Christian thinking.[2]

Importantly, Bourgeois Christians are not Cartesian in the philosophical sense, but rather in a common, existential sense. Descartes's

---

1. Gillespie, *Nihilism Before Nietzsche*, 1.
2. Dreyfus and Taylor, *Retrieving Realism*, 92.

cogito, ergo sum is the starting point for describing the *cogito, ergo sum Christian*. The idea is that being a Christian for Bourgeois Christians is thinking the right things: I think Christianly, therefore I am a Christian. Consequently, the Cartesian dualism inherent in the *cogito, ergo sum* exalts the mind while the body suffers a deep discount. And when Christianity is mostly about the mind, then a disembodied, disengaged Christian life prevails. But this kind of intellectualism sounds like the Neoplatonist Plotinus who taught that mental states are more real than action.[3] Plotinus influenced Descartes, and by using Descartes's ideas focus, I will show how this works out in Bourgeois Christianity.[4]

Descartes is often called the father of modern philosophy. As Alexis de Tocqueville explained almost two hundred years ago, and it still applies: "America, then, is one of the countries in which Descartes is studied least but his precepts are respected most."[5] Descartes's precepts lead to disengagement, clericalism, and the undertow of worldliness because of his focus on thinking as the source of truth.

In his *Discourse on Method*, Descartes offers his famous *cogito, ergo sum* as the ultimate basis for proving reality. Descartes starts from a position of radical doubt to find an unassailable basis for truth, and he finds it in the undeniable fact that he thinks. As he explains: "And noticing that this truth—*I think, therefore I am*—was so firm and so certain that the most extravagant suppositions of the sceptics were unable to shake it, I judged that I could accept it without scruple as the first principle of the philosophy I was seeking."[6] For Descartes, we find truth in reason and the reasoning mind. If you want truth, put your mind to work; if you find truth, it will be in your mind.

Descartes describes the mind's supremacy in this way:

> From this I knew that I was a substance the whole essence or nature of which was merely to think, and which, in order to exist, needed no place and depended on no material thing. Thus this "I," that is, the soul through which I am what I am, is entirely distinct from the body, and is even easier to know than the body, and even if there were no body, the soul would not cease to be all that it is.[7]

---

3. Wallis, *Neoplatonism*, 62.
4. Wallis, *Neoplatonism*, 172–73.
5. Tocqueville, *Democracy in America*, 483.
6. Descartes, *Discourse on Method*, 17. Emphasis in original.
7. Descartes, *Discourse on Method*, 18.

Accordingly, because "the mind is completely different from the body," the body has a different mode of being.[8] In fact, the mind does not need the body.

For Descartes there is the *res cogitans*—the thinking thing—and the *res extensa*—the body and everything outside the mind, which includes people. These two modes of being form a dualism, Descartes's mind/body dualism. The mind is primary, and the body is secondary. Consequently, people are primarily nonmaterial beings, nonphysical, thinking souls. The thinking person is the subject, and everything else including other people are objects. (Descartes follows Aristotle's idea of the *animal rationale*, that people are thinking animals, meaning that thinking is the essential characteristic of human nature.)

As Descartes says in his "Letter to Mersenne" in July 1641: "I have demonstrated that the soul is nothing other than a thing that thinks; it is therefore impossible that we can ever think of anything without having at the same time the idea of our soul, as of a thing capable of thinking all that we think about."[9] Hence for Descartes, man's soul is for thinking, and it follows that Bourgeois Christians believe that their chief duty is to think biblically. Man's mind is the fountain of truth in Cartesian rationalism, while the body drifts in its own separate mode of being. But as French philosopher Maurice Merleau-Ponty, a critic of Descartes, says: "The body is the vehicle of being in the world, and having a body is, for a living creature, to be intervolved in a definite environment, to identify oneself with certain projects and be continually committed to them."[10] Merleau-Ponty's secular description of engagement similarly describes the sacred duty of Christians to work in God's kingdom.

Paradoxically, this learning emphasis often produces spiritual languishing. When Christians believe that the goal of the Christian life is learning and having correct biblical knowledge, and they also discount

---

8. Descartes, *Meditations on First Philosophy*, 59. Descartes also says: "But nevertheless, on the one hand I have a clear and distinct idea of myself, in so far as I am simply a thinking, non-extended thing; and on the other hand I have a distinct idea of body, in so far as this is simply an extended, non-thinking thing. And accordingly, it is certain that I am really distinct from my body, and can exist without it" (54).

9. Gillespie, *Nihilism Before Nietzsche*, 50.

10. Merleau-Ponty, *Phenomenology of Perception*, 94. Also: "Man taken as a concrete being is not a psyche joined to an organism, but the movement to and fro of existence which at one time allows itself to take corporeal form and at others moves towards personal acts" (101).

service, they become the worldly Christian *res cogitans*—the Bourgeois Christians. This is a twenty-first-century version of Gnosticism, and Gnosticism is a religious dualism.

If we are the *res cogitans*, our job includes thinking and learning and also reasoning and organizing according to reason. We focus our minds on the Bible. This is commonly a good step, but for Bourgeois Christians it is a misstep. For the Christian *res cogitans*, being a Christian is a matter of consciousness, which means having the right biblical picture in the mind. You need the Christian mindset—the right ideas, the right picture in the mind. But this is a world-bent view the age holds captive.

Consciousness in this context means the human capacity to fill one's mind with information and process it. The Cartesian mind is like a container that holds ideas. If a biblical consciousness is the true end of the Christian life, then the goal becomes having all the theological furniture properly arranged in the rooms of the mind and making sure other Christians do too. But this means remodeling the Christian house as a worldly *res cogitans*.

Also, in Cartesian thinking, "the reality I want to know is outside the mind; my knowledge of it is within. This knowledge consists in states of mind which purport to represent accurately what is out there."[11] For the Cartesian, all meaning is an act of thought.[12] For the Cartesian consciousness, knowledge arises through these inner states called ideas, or inner representations, and they put me in contact with the world outside of me.[13]

This view supports a dangerous inner/outer mental structure of reality. Moreover, it follows that we have knowledge when our beliefs correspond reliably to reality, but that reality is on the outside, while how we know it is in the mind.[14] It is an inner picture of the outside world, and the inner picture is our reality. Now if the reader thinks this view is correct, that shows how strong the Cartesian world-picture holds sway. But to explain the problems with this view requires the rest of this book. First, however, it helps to describe some of the characteristics of the Cartesian world-picture.

---

11. Dreyfus and Taylor, *Retrieving Realism*, 2.

12. Merleau-Ponty, *Phenomenology of Perception*, 170.

13. Descartes's "representations" are not the same thing as the representations and ideas discussed in this book. I don't want to delve deeply into Descartes's epistemology and his understanding of how the mind works; however, Charles Taylor says that Descartes's representations "are perhaps best understood in contemporary terms as sentences held true" (*Secular Age*, 558). That explains much of what I am saying.

14. Dreyfus and Taylor, *Retrieving Realism*, 3.

For Descartes, there are four components of thinking that enable us to understand reality. First, we understand reality through the mind by way of representations, ideas, and beliefs held to be true. Second, we analyze knowledge as clearly defined elements or ideas that we have assembled or formulated, and this knowledge allows us to give an inventory of our beliefs. Third, these ideas stand as the proof of our beliefs and something we do not go beyond. Fourth, and very troubling, is the Cartesian dualism of the mental and the physical, the inner and the outer, the mind and the body.[15] Where and how are these four elements combined in Christian circles? What combines defining ideas or representations of truth that formulate and assemble an inventory of truths?[16]

We find three similar elements represented in historical statements like the Anglican Thirty-Nine Articles and the Presbyterian Westminster Confession of Faith. Both catalogue an inventory of fundamental biblical ideas. The ideas represent key elements of Christian truth and settle theological questions. They assemble the fundamental doctrines of the church in a document. They are truths to learn and keep in one's mind as guides. Importantly, they are products of early modern rationalism. Are these documents bad because they embrace three elements of Cartesian thinking? No. In fact, they can be very helpful. But when the fourth element—Cartesian dualism—joins with the first three, Christian truth stalls out in life and dives into worldliness. It becomes moralistic therapeutic theism.

Ideas, theology, and doctrine, representations of Christian truth, become more important than neighbors. Whether church members follow them or not, they symbolize what Christian truth is for Bourgeois Christians—a collection of biblical ideas. They describe how to understand truth. They focus on the mind and knowledge.

For example, I heard a PCA elder say that "Presbyterianism is mostly about doctrine." If it is mostly about doctrine, it is mostly about ideas or representations of Christian truth, which I will later describe as abstractions and generalizations. But standing alone in the detached mind, these truths end up as unsituated thought. Indeed, the twentieth-century ethicist Emmanuel Levinas notes, "Without the signification they draw from

---

15. Dreyfus and Taylor, *Retrieving Realism*, 2–3.

16. I am not using the word "representations" in Descartes's epistemological sense that describes the mind's operation. One philosophy professor describes Descartes's view of the mind as a homunculus inside a camera obscura with no direct knowledge of the external world: Ihde, *Bodies in Technology*, 72–73.

ethics theological concepts remain empty and formal frameworks."[17] Furthermore, if Presbyterianism is mostly about ideas, it bankrupts believers into the court of theological correctness that results in disembodied relationships. It transfers truth as existence to truth as exegesis. Truth resides in the thinking mind detached from the body.

The same elder said that "Christianity, and thus Calvinism, emphasizes doctrine. Religions emphasize experience. Doctrine involves thinking. Experience involves feeling." This elder separates the mind from feeling. He separates orthodoxy from action and passion. He unwittingly denies the book of Psalms that exalts feelings about the glory of God. The Psalms say: "The sound of joyful shouting and salvation is in the tents of the righteous" (Ps 118:15). Or, "Bless the Lord, O my soul, and all that is within me, bless His holy name" (Ps 103:1). Or, "Shout joyfully to the Lord, all the earth. Serve the Lord with gladness" (Ps 100:1–2). Or, "O sing to the Lord a new song, for He has done wonderful things" (Ps 98:1). These are all profound and exultant expressions of feelings. Would King David go to a church that disapproves of expressing his joy about God or a church that has anthropomorphized God into a theologian? This elder's words express the theological correctness of the Cartesian mind/body dualism.

What occupies the mind is what determines the truth for Cartesian rationalists and the truth about being a Christian for Bourgeois Christians. In this they follow the spirit of the age. As Martin Heidegger observed three hundred years after Descartes's *Discourse on Method*: "It always tends to be pointed out as a particular characteristic that modernity since Descartes no longer starts from the existence of God or from proofs of God, but from consciousness, from the I."[18] (This should remind you of the Sinner's Prayer of American revivalism.) This focus on the I and consciousness is part of the spirit of the age.

An obvious rejoinder to this argument is that Evangelicals find truth in God's revelation with the help of reason and the Holy Spirit. But what becomes of this revelation? Does it spark the believer's heart and grow hands and feet and walk about loving neighbors and serving God? Or does it become ideas populating a correct consciousness like antiques filling a room? God's revelation generates a service culture; the Cartesian rationalist view produces the knowledge culture of Bourgeois Christianity. God's revelation generates a life ethic; Cartesian rationalism promotes a Christian etiquette

---

17. Levinas, *Totality and Infinity*, 79.
18. Heidegger, *Fundamental Concepts of Metaphysics*, 55.

of knowing what to say and how to appear pious. One stirs to act; the other begins and ends in biblical insight. And all this leads deeper into paradox.

Bourgeois Christians try to legitimate their comfortable Christianity with learning, and they forget that the Christian life is a race (Heb 12:1), a pilgrimage (1 Pet 2:11–12), a struggle (Eph 6:12), a battle (2 Tim 2:3). Learning is comfortable, but sanctification is worked out with fear and trembling (Phil 2:12). Christianity demands an incarnate, embodied life, and the embodied life must express God's power in the body. As the apostle Paul teaches, it is "always carrying about in the body the dying of Jesus, so that the life of Jesus also may be manifested in our body" (2 Cor 4:10). Paul is not describing the life of a Christian lapsed into theological correctness. Rather, theological correctness becomes an evangelical form of Gnosticism, because as Kierkegaard explains, "to give thinking supremacy over everything else is gnosticism."[19]

With this brief overview of Descartes's mind/body dualism and its effects, I move on to show how one of his critics has described the cost of this dualism. This critique also indirectly describes Bourgeois Christians and shows the paradoxes described in this book.

Charles Taylor, former professor of moral philosophy at Oxford University, wrote extensively on Descartes's influence in the late modern age. He argues that Cartesian rationalism "calls for disengagement from world and body and the assumption of an instrumental stance towards them. It is of the essence of reason, both speculative and practical, that it pushes us to disengage."[20] Moreover, the disengaged person is "free and rational to the extent that he has fully distinguished himself from the natural and social worlds, so that his identity is no longer to be defined in terms of what lies outside him in these worlds."[21] Think of disengaged as disembodied and aloof—a kind of spiritual atomism disconnected from the neighbors whom God calls Christians to love and the community where he calls them to be salt and light. At least one Calvinist has seen these problems in Reformed churches.

Professor Paul Helm, a Reformed theologian and philosopher, has witnessed the loss of the Christian calling:

> This loss is partly a cause and partly a result of the present impotence, and derives from the idea that people are primarily

---

19. Kierkegaard, *Concluding Unscientific Postscript*, 1:341.
20. Taylor, *Sources of the Self*, 155.
21. Taylor, *Philosophical Arguments*, 7.

non-material beings with non-material needs and throw-away bodies.... Men and women are souls to be saved, and no more. And because we think in these abstract yet individualistic ways we never come to think concretely about how the faith that, say, a businessman professes is to affect his business, or that of a student his studies.[22]

That people are primarily nonmaterial beings is the Cartesian view. That people are only souls to be saved is the easy-believism gospel view. This leads to an "understanding of faith as private and psychological."[23] The private and psychological faith operates in the mind and not with bodies embedded in a community. This is the Cartesian consciousness of Bourgeois Christianity.

Contrast this view with the biblical calling. The Christian is a creature of God, living in the creation of God, subject to the authority of God, in vital union with God, and in a covenantal relationship with him. This is primordially an ethical relationship carried out by faith and empowered by God's grace through the Holy Spirit. The Christian's social world is communal because the Christian is a member of and has responsibilities for the kingdom of God, fellow believers, and neighbors. These relationships define the Christian's identity and impose duties. They are ethical relationships. There is no dualism and no inner/outer realm with the inner being the true being.

Taylor further says that Cartesian dualism creates the buffered self and its egocentricity. "For the modern, buffered self, the possibility exists of taking a distance from, disengaging from everything outside the mind. My ultimate purposes are those which arise within me, the crucial meanings of things are those defined in my responses to them."[24] This buffered self is the product of modern reason. The *res cogitans* isolates itself from the *res extensa*. The mind processes and interprets reality, and it does this because of the mind's self-sufficiency. "The buffered self is essentially the self which is aware of the possibility of disengagement. And disengagement is frequently carried out in relation to one's whole surroundings, natural and social."[25] Bourgeois Christians buffer themselves from their neighbors.

---

22. Helm, "Christian Man's Calling," 21.
23. Helm, "Christian Man's Calling," 22.
24. Taylor, *Secular Age*, 38.
25. Taylor, *Secular Age*, 42.

Taylor further describes Descartes's influence in this way: "This powerful model of all-around disengagement gets handed down in the tradition of modernity; not indeed, without contestation, but with a tremendous power attaching to it."[26] The disengaged style of the buffered self is a widespread mode of existence and a common perspective about life in America and in Evangelicalism.

Accordingly, I describe Bourgeois Christianity philosophically like this: because it is Cartesian, it is a paganized Christianity in which Bourgeois Christians retain Christian metaphysics (doctrine) but reject Christian ethics.[27] They think doctrine and neglect duty. Thinking waxes and working wanes, while true biblical understanding is eclipsed. In this way, Bourgeois Christians define themselves as Christians based on what is in their minds. Christian learning swells while Christian doing fades. This drains the Christian life of vitality. This mode of receiving Christian truth is not a biblical mode because it "understands" the words but squanders the power and neglects the duty.

This focus on the mind smacks of a kind of empty Neoplatonism that seeks higher truth and eschews the duties of the body. Plotinus describes the Neoplatonic goal this way: "Wisdom is an intellectual activity which turns away from the things below and leads the soul to those above. So the soul when it is purified becomes form and formative power, altogether bodiless and intellectual and entirely belonging to the divine."[28] And when the believer's goal becomes seeking the higher truths of theology and doctrine or the nuances of the apocalypse, he or she is unwittingly influenced by pagan thought. Consequently, the paradox of the disembodied world of Bourgeois Christianity is the dumbing-down of the kingdom of God in the name of the kingdom of God.

---

26. Taylor, *Secular Age*, 285.
27. Westphal, *Kierkegaard's Critique of Reason*, 44.
28. Plotinus, *Porphyry on Plotinus*, 251.

Chapter 7 Kierkegaard on Subjectivity and Nietzsche on the Emptiness of the Age

Two critics of the modern age show the emptiness and worldliness of an intellectualist Christianity. One is a believer, and one is an atheist.

Søren Kierkegaard, a believer, spent his life rebuking the complacency and formalism of the mid-nineteenth-century Danish church. Although he rarely mentions Descartes,[1] he scorned consciousness-as-reality as a plague on the church. Kierkegaard understood the depth of the knowledge problem, and he also understood it as a modern-age problem. He warns that "because of much knowledge people have entirely forgotten what it means to *exist* and what *inwardness* is."[2]

Kierkegaard does not talk about embodiment. He uses the word "subjectivity" as the way to overcome the knowledge problem and the lethargy that it creates. And in describing subjectivity, he explains that "existing is

---

1. Here is an example of when Kierkegaard does mention Descartes: "The Cartesian *cogito ergo sum* [I think therefore I am] has been repeated often enough. If the I in *cogito* is understood to be an individual human being, then the statement demonstrates nothing: I *am* thinking ergo I am, but if I *am* thinking, no wonder, then, that I am; after all, it has already been said, and the first consequently says even more than the last. If, then, by the I in *cogito*, one understands a single individual existing human being, philosophy shouts: Foolishness, foolishness, here it is not a matter of my *I* or your *I* but of the pure *I*. But surely this pure *I* can have no other existence than thought-existence. What, then, is the concluding formula supposed to mean; indeed, there is no conclusion, for then the statement is a tautology" (*Concluding Unscientific Postscript*, 1:317). Emphasis in original.

2. Kierkegaard, *Concluding Unscientific Postscript*, 1:242. Emphasis in original.

something quite different from knowing."[3] Maurice Merleau-Ponty likewise notes that "the true *Cogito* does not define the subject's existence in terms of the thought he has of existing."[4] Bourgeois Christians do this: they define themselves by how they think about being a Christian.

Kierkegaard warns the person of faith that "much fear and trembling will be needed lest he fall into temptation and confuse knowledge with faith."[5] The subjectivity of faith must overcome the trap of the abstractions of objective knowledge. And for Kierkegaard, subjectivity is more than insight into biblical truth.

It is easy to misunderstand Kierkegaard's idea of subjectivity by confusing it with contemporary notions of "subjective truth." He did not believe that "what is true for you is true for you, and what is true for me is true for me." He did not believe that there is no truth except personal truth. He did not deny the objective reality of the incarnation, the crucifixion, or the resurrection of Jesus. Indeed, he affirmed these biblical events and others.[6] So by subjectivity, he does not mean that truth is subjective as many understand it today.

For Kierkegaard truth as subjectivity means that Christian truth is seized by the heart and exercised in the life. Truth is not facts organized in the mind; truth rallies the heart, and the heart makes up the whole person. The inwardness of Christian truth, if you have it, compels outwardness. Subjective truth is life-changing truth, not a philosophical theory or theological system, but truth acted out in life.[7] It is existential. Believers drink from the cup of grace and pour out love.[8]

Again, Kierkegaard did not deny the truth of the gospel, and doctrine is not the problem. But teaching must awaken the believer's life.[9] Indeed, he emphasizes the potency of biblical truth and how believers should have changed lives. Martin Luther embodied this inwardness and passion by challenging the corrupt practices of the Catholic Church.[10] Abraham

---

3. Kierkegaard, *Concluding Unscientific Postscript*, 1:297.
4. Merleau-Ponty, *Phenomenology of Perception*, xiv.
5. Kierkegaard, *Concluding Unscientific Postscript*, 1:29.
6. See, for example, Kierkegaard, *Concept of Anxiety*, 162.
7. Kierkegaard, *Concluding Unscientific Postscript*, 1:371.
8. Kierkegaard, *Concluding Unscientific Postscript*, 1:192.
9. Kierkegaard, *Concluding Unscientific Postscript*, 1:379.
10. Kierkegaard, *Concluding Unscientific Postscript*, 1:341.

acted in faith by leaving his homeland and his people.[11] For Kierkegaard, Christianity as correct consciousness is paganism, or as he explains it, "To know a creed by rote is paganism because Christianity is inwardness."[12] An outworking of love follows the inworking of grace, and this spiritual power was absent in the Danish Church during Kierkegaard's life.

Kierkegaard's age was much like today. "In an age of knowledge, in which all are Christians and know what Christianity is, it is only all too easy to use the holy names without meaning anything thereby, to rattle off the Christian truth without having the least impression of it."[13] This is godtalk. In a vivid way, he says that Christian talk had become a toothless maundering like an old man without teeth.[14] The church is the toothless old man. Yet God promises to make his people "into a threshing sledge, new and sharp, with many teeth. You will thresh the mountains and crush them and reduce the hills to chaff" (Isa 41:15 NIV). Today, as in Kierkegaard's time, most Evangelicals have lost this power.

When Kierkegaard lived in Denmark, most Danes belonged to the state church and claimed to be Christians, but their faith didn't inspire works. As secularism's waves have swept over America, most people don't claim to be Christians, but Bourgeois Christians still rattle off Christian truth that has little power in their lives. Evangelists often use biblical terms empty of meaning to get "decisions"—a change of consciousness about sin, self, and Jesus. Having eternal life means going to heaven when you die. Consequently, the shallowness and formalism of the mid-nineteenth-century Danish Church lives on in the spiritual smugness of many Evangelicals. And as Kierkegaard explains, Christianity without subjectivity lacks inwardness and passion and is heartless.

Kierkegaard describes this kind of Christianity as one that turns Christians into onlookers, not kingdom workers. It leads to a life of Christian reflection, not loving action. He explains that "modern thought tends to reduce being to thinking."[15] This is the Cartesian consciousness and the Cartesian influence. The Rom 12:2 command to transform one's

---

11. See generally Kierkegaard, *Fear and Trembling*.
12. Kierkegaard, *Concluding Unscientific Postscript*, 1:224.
13. Kierkegaard, *Concluding Unscientific Postscript*, 1:283.
14. Kierkegaard, *Concluding Unscientific Postscript*, 1:363. This reminds me of Alexis de Tocqueville's criticism of the kind of people democracy produces: "People feel desire, regret, sorrow, and joy, but nothing visible or lasting comes of it, much as the passion of an old man culminates in impotence and nothing more" (*Democracy in America*, 11).
15. Dupré, "Sickness unto Death," 86.

mind lapses into filling the mind with biblical facts and developing the correct doctrinal picture. This leaches the riches of being a Christian out of Christianity. This is, in part, what Ludwig Wittgenstein describes as picture holding us captive.[16]

Kierkegaard further explains: "Because faith, hope, and love, because God and Jesus Christ are talked about in church in a solemn voice . . . , it still by no means follows that this is a godly address. The decisive point is how the speaker and the listeners relate themselves to the discourse or are presumed to relate themselves to it."[17] In other words, what effect does the message have on church members? Understanding this effect is especially confusing when the aesthetic infiltrates the church and infects hearers. The word preached can leave the hearers with a small dose of orthodoxy but no service.

Dr. Paul David Tripp, formerly of Westminster Seminary, makes a similar point. He explains the difference between faith and amazement. Faith radically changes a believer's life. But someone can be "amazed" with God's plan of salvation, or the apocalypse, or the preaching at church. (Amazement is a manifestation of the aesthetic.) Amazement, however, is not faith because amazement is not life changing. As Tripp notes, "[God] is not satisfied with the wonder of our minds. He will not relent until he has established his life-altering rule in our hearts."[18] The life-altering rule is an ethical rule that the aesthetic obstructs.

For example, one hundred church members can go on a weekend retreat, hear the Bible preached, and think that it is "amazing." Yet for many, their experience never rises above the charm of the aesthetic. Because the Bible is taught does not mean someone's experience in hearing it taught is a spiritual experience. This is a common misunderstanding among Evangelicals. In an aesthetic hearing, the Bourgeois Christian gains only a temporal knowledge of eternal truth. They may come away with new insight but lack the will to act. The fellowship they enjoy may be only aesthetic. This wonder or pleasure or amazement of things spiritual is often just a twenty-first-century version of what Kierkegaard calls the aesthetic view of Christianity.

J. C. Ryle, an evangelical Anglican bishop, describes the aesthetic well:

> When the Gospel of Christ is placed before a man's soul, it is as
> if God offered to him a lighted candle. It is not sufficient to hear

---

16. Wittgenstein, *Philosophical Investigations*, 53.
17. Kierkegaard, *Concluding Unscientific Postscript*, 1:418, unnumbered note.
18. Tripp, *New Morning Mercies*, June 27.

it, and assent to it, and admire it, and acknowledge its truth. It must be received into the heart, and obeyed in the life. Until this takes place the Gospel does him no more good than if he were an African heathen, who has never heard the Gospel at all.[19]

Orthodoxy is not enough. The aesthetic is not enough. The gospel message requires the subjectivity of pathos.

Pathos is the feelings and emotions that infuse life with vitality. In the Christian life, the believer needs passion. And for Kierkegaard there are two kinds of pathos, aesthetic pathos and existential pathos: "The aesthetic pathos distances itself from existence or is present in it through an illusion, whereas the existential pathos immerses itself in existing, pierces all illusions with the consciousness of existing, and becomes more and more concrete by acting to transform existence."[20] The true believer has existential pathos. As Kierkegaard's book *Works of Love* shows, that means loving your neighbor sacrificially.

I can describe the aesthetic pathos with the example of the good sermon that pleases Bourgeois Christians. The preacher explains his three points, he bases the sermon on a biblical text, he uses proper exegesis, he stays within the bounds of correct doctrine, and he tells interesting stories. Bourgeois Christians enjoy the sermon, it gives them pleasure, they understand it, it adds to their knowledge, and they feel good when they leave the pews. But it ends there until they come back next Sunday for the next sermon.

Bourgeois Christians enjoy pastors who preach well, but in their preaching, too many pastors demand little from the congregation. They thereby promote the aesthetic understanding of Scripture. But the aesthetic pathos begins and ends with interest, enjoyment, and satisfaction, and Bourgeois Christians enjoy this peace-filling satisfaction. A good sermon satisfies them. But with existential pathos, the sermon changes them. It transforms, and it should transform into what Kierkegaard calls concrete action.

Becoming more concrete and transforming your existence means embodying truth. It requires embedding in a community, not just going to church. But Bourgeois Christians distance themselves from this concrete, immersed, and embedded style of living. Importantly, Kierkegaard says that the Christianity of aesthetic pathos is an illusion. In other words,

---

19. Ryle, *Luke 11–24*, 37.
20. Kierkegaard, *Concluding Unscientific Postscript*, 1:432.

this religious formalism of stunted orthodoxy deludes Bourgeois Christians who reflect on it but don't act on it. It gives them a false confidence about their salvation.

Kierkegaard ends his important work *Concluding Unscientific Postscript to Philosophical Fragments* with this statement: "Since the highest is to become and to continue to be a Christian, the task cannot be to reflect on Christianity but can only be to intensify by means of reflection the pathos with which one continues to be a Christian."[21] Passion, pathos, or the feeling of urgency in the Christian life is largely absent among many Evangelicals. Reflection, by which Kierkegaard means learning the faith and thinking about it but not acting on it, leads to the wood, hay, and stubble of a feet-hobbling faith. Sagacity controls reflection, and this shrewdness yields procrastination and indecision about working for God.[22]

But contrary to the age, true faith stirs up action. "Certainly true faith in Jesus always will result in action," says twentieth-century Calvinist J. Gresham Machen.[23] Martin Heidegger, however, says it better: "True understanding never proves its mettle in repeating something after someone, but only in its power to lead understanding into genuine action, into objective achievement."[24] If Kierkegaard were here today, he would ask Evangelicals: Has an infinite and eternal change happened in your life?

Friedrich Nietzsche, the unbeliever, died in 1900, almost fifty years after Kierkegaard's death. Although his writing swells and fades from trenchant insight to bombast, he identified some of the same problems that Kierkegaard saw: lack of passion and little concrete action and objective achievement. Nietzsche says that "the most characteristic quality of modern man [is]: the remarkable antithesis between an interior which fails to correspond to any exterior and an exterior which fails to correspond to any interior—an antithesis unknown to the peoples of earlier times."[25]

Nietzsche is another witness against a central trait of Bourgeois Christians. They have an interior, their minds, filled with biblical knowledge; but the exterior, their bodies, do not transfer this knowledge into loving their neighbors. They live in the comfortable inner world of their consciousness. This is not new. Over one hundred years ago, philosopher Alfred North

21. Kierkegaard, *Concluding Unscientific Postscript*, 1:607.
22. Kierkegaard, *Upbuilding Discourses*, 113.
23. Machen, *What Is Faith?*, 89.
24. Heidegger, *Fundamental Concepts of Metaphysics*, 300.
25. Nietzsche, *Untimely Meditations*, 78.

Whitehead observed that "religion is tending to degenerate into a decent formula wherewith to embellish a comfortable life."[26] These embellishments are aesthetic, part of the Bourgeois Christian knowledge culture, and this goes back to Nietzsche and how he describes his age:

> This precisely is why our modern culture is not a living thing: . . . it is not a real culture at all but only a kind of knowledge of culture; it has an idea of and feeling for culture but no true cultural achievement emerges from them. What actually inspires it and then appears as a visible act, on the other hand, often signifies not much more than an indifferent convention, a pitiful imitation or even a crude caricature.[27]

But unlike Bourgeois Christians, Nietzsche knew what the Christian life demanded, and he hated it. He recognized that "from the start, the Christian faith is a sacrifice."[28] He hated this call to sacrifice because he thought it turned people into herd animals, degenerated them, and made them timid and tame.[29] (Incidentally, Nietzsche admired Jesus.)

Nietzsche's view of Christianity as a religion of sacrifice makes him a strange bedfellow with John Calvin. In one of the strongest passages from the *Institutes of the Christian Religion*, Calvin says:

> Hence it is very clear that we keep the commandments not by loving ourselves but by loving God and neighbor; that he lives the best and holiest life who lives and strives for himself as little as he can, and that no one lives in a worse or more evil manner than he who lives and strives for himself alone, and thinks about and seeks only his own advantage.[30]

Sacrifice—how contrary to the spirit of our democratic, therapeutic, individualistic age.

Paradoxically, one of the greatest enemies of Christianity and one of its greatest champions agree on what Bourgeois Christians miss with their disembodied Christian lives. They miss the concrete. They have an inside but no outside. This disengaged Christianity encourages a self-centered spirituality that can't break out of the castles of their minds and cross the

---

26. Whitehead, *Science and the Modern World*, 188.
27. Nietzsche, *Untimely Meditations*, 78.
28. Nietzsche, *Beyond Good and Evil*, 60.
29. Nietzsche, *Beyond Good and Evil*, 111.
30. Calvin, *Institutes*, 1:417.

moats of doctrine to love neighbors while fighting off the slings and arrows of the world. This emptiness is part of the modern age.

In this chapter and the previous chapter, I describe the paradox that a lifetime of learning the Bible can lead to a Christian life empty of service. Believing that having good theology and sound doctrine makes one a good Christian can lead to a lifelong sabbatical from kingdom work. An essential part of explaining this paradox is to show that it is worldly and part of the spirit of modernity. The apostle Paul and the New Testament writers in general did "not describe the growth of faith in terms of its psychological development."[31] This is Cartesian, and as Calvin says, faith is not a matter of assent.[32] Faith is a matter of the heart.

---

31. Rudolf Bultmann, "πιστεύω," *TDNT* 6:174–228, esp. 6:217.
32. Calvin, *Institutes*, 1:552.

Chapter 8 The Centrality of the Heart

IF THE CARTESIAN CONSCIOUSNESS is worldly and fuels worldliness among Evangelicals, how does one remedy this feeble consciousness? If this mind focus creates a gaunt and trembling Christian witness, on what should believers focus? The answer is the heart. Biblical thinking and biblical living come from the heart because, according to the Bible, Christians think with their hearts. How odd to modern ears!

This chapter and the next share an important premise: the modern understanding of the mind has displaced the biblical concept of the heart and how it guides and unites a person's life. Among other problems, this produces worldliness, clericalism, and theological correctness.

It is a mistake to believe that a twenty-first-century person understands the world the same way someone understood it two thousand years ago. Similarly, it is a mistake to think we understand some biblical words the way Christians in the first century understood them. St. Paul's Letter to the Romans offers an example of the confusion.

In Rom 10:10, Paul writes that "with the heart a person believes, resulting in righteousness, and with the mouth he confesses, resulting in salvation." Paul describes believing as a matter of the heart, not the mind. But if we reflect on how we talk about the heart and mind today, we believe with the mind and feel with the heart. For moderns the mind is the source of reason and thought and where we process and store information. It is the seat of judgment where we weigh different ideas to find the correct one or consider different plans to choose the best one. On the other hand, we refer to the heart when describing our emotions, feelings, and intuitions.

In the modern age, we do not feel with our minds, and we do not think with our hearts. They have separate functions. Calvinist theologian

Charles Hodge says that "it is no uncommon thing to find men having two theologies,—one of the intellect, and another of the heart."[1] Here Hodge explains in one sentence the lesson of this book: Bourgeois Christians have a sound theology for their intellects and a body-comfortable theology for their hearts, where action begins.

Indeed, the difference between our modern understanding of heart and mind is often expressed as the two in conflict. They have different functions. For example, we say, "My mind is telling me to do one thing, but my heart is telling me to do something else." In other words, my reasoning mind, after thoughtful consideration, is telling me to act one way; but my heart, my feelings, intuitions, or passions, is telling me to do the opposite. So what does the Bible say about the heart?

Heart in the Bible is a metaphor, a figure of speech, that tells us about human powers and actions. The metaphorical character of the word "heart" implies limits to what we can know about it. Mysteries abound in the Bible, and mysteries require metaphors to help us understand. If you want to know about the heart inside your chest, a cardiologist can explain how it works. But doctors and scientists cannot describe the realm of spirit where the biblical heart pumps. Well-meaning, orthodox theologians have applied logic and reason to biblical texts, but many mysteries remain, and the heart is one of them.

As a biblical metaphor, heart has much function but no anatomy. It is centrally important but mysteriously allusive in form. Consequently, this chapter on the heart is more about admonition than definition. Too much focus on a word's meaning can end in a haze that hinders understanding. Too often definitions are not as definitive or helpful as many theologians believe. One must look at the use and the context of the word. Indeed, theology is like a series of family snapshots that shows us the family but tells us little about it. On occasion it helps to look away from the theological use of words to their everyday use because we live in the everyday. Indeed, definitions too often become Cartesian, meaning that once Bourgeois Christians learn the definition of something, they think their duty ends there. But this kind of learning is like riding on a carousel that leads Bourgeois Christians to believe that because they are moving, they are going somewhere in the Christian life, yet they are only going in circles.

---

1. Hodge, *Systematic Theology*, 1:16.

From the existential, everyday standpoint, however, the heart is not a place in a believer; it is a direction for a believer. The heart is a matter of spirit. How the Bible uses the word "heart" is very complex.

The *Theological Dictionary of the New Testament*[2] describes the use and importance of the word "heart," or *kardia*, in all its complexity in the Old and New Testaments. Heart occurs 850 times as a word describing people. Most importantly, it represents the totality of a person's life and the vitality of that person's spirit.[3] The Bible describes a unity of personhood based in the heart, not the modern-age division between mind and heart or mind and body. We especially see this unity in the Old Testament.

In the Old Testament, the heart is the innermost part of a person. It is what God sees while everyone else sees only outward appearances.[4] Specifically with reference to thinking, the heart is the seat of mental and spiritual powers.[5] For example, "Do not oppress the widow or the orphan, the stranger or the poor; and do not devise evil in your hearts against one another" (Zech 7:10). In the Bible the heart, not the mind, devises evil. Today, however, we say that a person who devises evil has an evil mind. On the other hand, and biblically speaking, when a person is faithful to God, that person is doing what accords with God's heart (1 Sam 2:35). God seeks those whose hearts follow after his heart, and that means obeying his commandments (1 Sam 13:14).[6]

The heart is also the seat of rational functions and understanding.[7] Even though the Israelites had seen signs and wonders, that seeing had not transformed their hearts. They failed to understand in the biblical sense—meaning with their hearts. No doubt the Israelites could describe what they saw, but neither accurately describing nor correctly explaining

---

2. *TDNT* has suffered some serious criticism. The biggest problem seems to be failing to come to grips with understanding biblical words in their context. I am careful to contextualize the words, for example in ch. 10 on *aletheia*. I generally follow the approach outlined in an article written by RTS Professor Steven M. Baugh, who says that Kittel can be used with profit by biblical theologians, and it is a vast Bible resource ("Kittel and Biblical Theology").

3. Karl-Wolfgang Troger, "ψυχή," *TDNT* 9:608–66, esp. 9:626.

4. Johannes Behm, "καρδία," *TDNT* 3:605–13, esp. 3:606. See also 1 Sam 16:7.

5. Behm, *TDNT* 3:606.

6. "But now your kingdom shall not endure. The Lord has sought out for Himself a man after His own heart, and the Lord has appointed him as ruler over His people, because you have not kept what the Lord commanded you."

7. Behm, *TDNT* 3:606.

equals spiritual discerning or devoted living. They understood it aesthetically. Stated another way, someone can describe an event, explain an idea, or understand a concept but miss the spiritual reality, which means the working reality. Spiritual reality is a biblical understanding rooted in a heart that bears fruit. This is an existential understanding, and it is truth held in passionate subjectivity.

Biblical thoughts root in the heart, bloom in the life, and cultivate the fruit of love. For example, in admonishing the young man to observe his parents' teachings, Prov 6:21–22 reads, "Bind them continually on your heart; / Tie them around your neck. / When you walk about, they will guide you; / When you sleep, they will watch over you; / And when you awake, they will talk to you." This is the Christian existential understanding of heart poetically described.

When God tells the Israelites to cast off their old sins and be renewed, he admonishes them to "make yourselves a new heart and a new spirit!" (Ezek 18:31). Proverbs 4:23 offers another vivid metaphor about the heart: "Watch over your heart with all diligence, for from it flow the springs of life." But there is more to the biblical view of the heart.

Planning and volition also come from the heart.[8] Solomon says that it was in his father David's heart to build the temple (1 Kgs 8:17). Indeed, the heart stirs the will to act: "Now set your heart and your soul to seek the Lord your God; arise, therefore, and build the sanctuary of the Lord God" (1 Chron 22:19). "Ezra had set his heart to study the law of the Lord and to practice it, and to teach His statutes and ordinances in Israel" (Ezra 7:10). Likewise, Daniel "purposed in his heart that he would not defile himself" (Dan 1:8 KJV). God's children make plans in their hearts, and the will to carry out those plans also comes from the heart. Christian action requires the will to do, and that will comes from the heart.

"Religious and moral conduct is rooted in the heart."[9] Samuel warns the Israelites to turn from evil and "serve the Lord with all your heart" (1 Sam 12:20). A heart that does not serve God must be circumcised, and that means radically transformed. The believer obeys God's commandments with the heart (Prov 7:1–3), and with the heart the believer is strong in the faith (Ps 27:14). Importantly, God blesses the pure in heart (Ps 24:4–5), but he hates the perverse in heart (Prov 11:20). Used here, the word "heart" stands for the whole person. There is no Cartesian dualism.

---

8. Behm, *TDNT* 3:607.
9. Behm, *TDNT* 3:607.

The New Testament follows the Old Testament understanding of the heart. The New Testament focuses "on the heart as the main organ of psychic and spiritual life, the place in man [where] God bears witness to Himself."[10] Foolish men are those who are "slow of heart to believe" (Luke 24:25). Moreover, doubts arise from the heart, and when Jesus's disciples see him after the resurrection and are afraid, Jesus asks them, "Why are you troubled, and why do doubts arise in your hearts?" (Luke 24:38). Thoughts are in the heart, so when Simeon blesses Mary, he says, "And a sword will pierce even your own soul—to the end that thoughts from many hearts may be revealed" (Luke 2:35). Thinking happens in the heart, and Jesus had the power to know the thoughts in men's hearts. For example, "Jesus knowing their thoughts said, 'Why are you thinking evil in your hearts?'" (Matt 9:4).[11] Finally, Paul describes evil men as those who are futile in their speculations and have a foolish and darkened heart (Rom 1:21).

Consequently, "the heart is the centre of the inner life of man and the source or seat of all the forces and functions of soul and spirit."[12] The heart is the source of feelings, emotions, and desires. It is "the seat of understanding [and] the source of thought and reflection," and also of man's will.[13] When God's people cannot hear him, it is because their hearts have become dull (Matt 13:15). Indeed, they cannot understand truth because their hearts have been hardened (John 12:40). "Thus the heart is supremely the one centre in man to which God turns, in which the religious life is rooted, which determines moral conduct."[14] This shows that the heart, not the mind of the Cartesian consciousness, is the center of the Christian life and that there is a unity of personhood—no mind/body dualism. The heart wills obedience and produces the fruit of the Spirit in the body. As Paul David Tripp explains, the heart is "the inner, spiritual, thoughtful, desiring, motivational you, . . . the *causal core of your personhood*."[15]

Parenthetically, looking again at Dan 1:8, I quoted that verse from the KJV and not the NASB like all the other verses. The KJV translates the passage as "purposed in his heart," but the NASB translates it as "made up his mind." The NASB uses "mind," and the KJV uses "heart." The NASB also

10. Behm, *TDNT* 3:611.
11. See also Luke 9:47.
12. Behm, *TDNT* 3:611.
13. Behm, *TDNT* 3:612.
14. Behm, *TDNT* 3:612.
15. Tripp, *New Morning Mercies*, June 11. Emphasis in original.

translates Prov 18:15 using the word "mind," while the KJV, the NIV, and the ESV use "heart." Proverbs 18:15 reads: "The heart of the discerning acquires knowledge; the ears of the wise seek it out" (NIV). "Mind" is also substituted for "heart" in the NASB translation of Jer 7:31. I suspect that substituting "mind" for "heart" in the NASB is designed to accommodate the modern understanding of the mind. I further suspect that this translation can mislead readers into the Cartesian trap. But now back to the importance of the word "heart" and the conclusion of this chapter.

In summary, the heart is the source and seat of thinking, will, desires, emotions, volition, and spiritual life. The heart unites the person, and there is no mind/body dualism. Christians love and serve God with their hearts, which means with every part of their being. Therefore, the Christian life is not primarily intellectual or in the mind; it engages daily-life feelings and emotions in heartfelt, heart-directed obedience.

Teaching is essential to cultivating the Christian fruits that grow from the soil of the heart. The biblical concept of teaching also shows the centrality of the heart because biblical teaching is supposed to change the whole person, not just the person's mind. Accordingly, the word "teaching," as used in the Septuagint, "always lays claim to the whole man and not merely to certain parts of him."[16] This unites personhood and community. Indeed, "the whole teaching of Jesus is with a view to the ordering of life with reference to God and one's neighbour."[17]

Thus, Jesus's teaching calls on the will seated in the heart, not the abstraction called the modern mind, and his call invokes the unity of personhood in the community of life. Hence, both the biblical concept of the heart and biblical teaching in general go far beyond theological correctness and a biblical consciousness or worldview. But as Tocqueville explained almost two hundred years ago about Christians in America: "They practice their religion accordingly, without shame and without weakness, yet even their zeal is usually suffused with something so tranquil, so methodical, and so calculated that what brings them to the foot of the altar would seem to be the head far more than the heart."[18] So the Bourgeois Christians' heart-at-the-expense-of-the-head problem is not new.

---

16. Karl Heinrich Rengstorf, "διδάσκω," *TDNT* 2:135–48, esp. 2:137.
17. Rengstorf, *TDNT* 2:140.
18. Tocqueville, *Democracy in America*, 615–16.

But confusing the mind with the heart is not the Bourgeois Christians' only spiritual anatomy problem. Closely related is the problem of the eyes versus the ears or seeing versus hearing.

Chapter 9 Seeing-as-Understanding versus Hearing-then-Doing

THE LAST CHAPTER EXPLAINED heart versus mind. This chapter describes seeing versus hearing as two different ways of understanding. It explains what seeing-as-understanding is and how it describes Bourgeois Christians' unbiblical thinking. It shows the pagan roots of seeing-as-understanding in Plato and Aristotle. This mode of understanding also characterizes the aesthete's view of Christianity, which fits the Bourgeois Christians' view of piety that mimics our aesthetic age. In contrast, I describe hearing-then-doing, the biblical answer to pagan thinking, and how hearing-then-doing leads to an existential Christianity. First, consider how we use the word "seeing."

Although we think about seeing as something our eyes do, in common talk we use seeing as a word for understanding. For example, you explain something to someone and then ask, "Do you see what I mean?" Or, "Do you see how this works?" Or, "Do you see where I'm going with this argument?" "Seeing" in these questions is synonymous with understanding. But this is not just common usage; it is ancient and goes back more than two thousand years to the Greek view of truth.

Conversely, think of hearing as a kind of understanding. What do you say when you want a child to obey? To the three-year-old, you say, "Close the door." Or, "Leave your sister alone." Or, "Don't talk to me like that." Or to your employee, you say, "Have the job finished by Friday." In the religious context of command and obedience, hearing requires doing, and seeing-as-understanding cannot satisfy or substitute for the hearing-then-doing command.

Furthermore, doing follows hearing in an ethical setting and in relationships involving different levels of authority like God and his people. And most importantly, hearing-then-doing is the vital and prevailing kind of knowing in the Bible. For example, "Hear, O Israel! The Lord is our God, the Lord is one!" (Deut 6:4). "Hear, O Israel, the statutes and the ordinances which I am speaking today in your hearing, that you may learn them and observe them carefully" (Deut 5:1). "Hear the word of the Lord" (Jer 2:4). And, "O Israel, you should listen and be careful to do it, that it may be well with you" (Deut 6:3). Fundamentally, this call to hear includes the call to act.

In a sense, seeing is a pagan way of understanding, and hearing is the biblical way. But biblical hearing is a special kind of hearing that engages intellect, will, and body in action, which means biblical hearing hears with the heart and works through the body. Paul shows the centrality of hearing when he says, "So faith comes from hearing, and hearing by the word of Christ" (Rom 10:17). Bourgeois Christians, on the other hand, follow the pagan seeing-as-understanding of the Cartesian consciousness that leads to the mind/body dualism—a knowing bereft of doing. The Bourgeois Christians' mode of understanding is a seeing and therefore optical. In this mode of understanding, the learning ends when Bourgeois Christians know biblical truths and what they mean. But this knowing is understood in a Greek way, not in a biblical way. This optical pattern is more pagan than Christian.

It helps to look closer at the pagan seeing-as-understanding and how the ancient Greeks understood knowing and knowledge, contrasted with how hearing is used in the Old and New Testaments. For the ancient Greeks, the eye was more reliable than the ear. They understood knowledge as knowledge of what really is and therefore something to be verified.[1] Indeed, Aristotle begins his *Metaphysics* by saying that "of all the senses sight best helps us to know things, and reveals many distinctions."[2] Accordingly, knowledge comes from observing and reflecting. Knowledge implies disclosure and insight, and one gains it by inspecting from the outside as an observer. It follows that "any participation in what is known is limited to seeing."[3] Note the importance of insight and observing from

---

1. Rudolf Bultmann, "γινώσκω," *TDNT* 1:689–714, esp. 1:691.
2. Aristotle, *Metaphysics*, 3.
3. Bultmann, *TDNT* 1:691.

without—that is, with objective truth seen and understood, but not necessarily inspiring works of love.

Seeing-as-understanding is a kind of grasping or comprehending, and for the Greeks, understanding comes from the seeing mind.[4] Understanding is grasping the true reality of the cosmos and not letting the everyday world of appearances hide reality. This demands correct thinking, making proper distinctions, and properly organizing ideas. Aristotle uses this approach in his works. Plato uses the dialectical method to reach the same end, and Plato's cave allegory offers a good example of the power of seeing as understanding for Greek thinkers.[5]

In Plato's allegory, prisoners are tethered together and living in a cave. All they can see are shadows on the cave wall in front of them, and they believe that the shadows are truth. But the shadows come from a fire behind them that they cannot see. Their captors carry artifacts along a path behind the prisoners but in front of the fire to cast the shadows. The captors deceive the prisoners into believing that the shadows are reality and that they are seeing truth, so the shadows are the only reality they know. (Interestingly, John Calvin agrees with Plato that human life is like smoke or shadow.[6])

For Plato the cave symbolizes the everyday world of appearances and mere opinions devoid of truth. To know true reality, one must escape from the cave, climb out into the blazing light of the true world, and see the Form of the Good that establishes truth. Plato uses the cave allegory to show that most people live as prisoners bound together in the cave of the world of appearances looking at shadows, not truth. They are deceived and self-deceived at the same time. The philosopher is the one who climbs out of the cave into the shining light of the Form of the Good to see truth.

According to Plato, coming out of the cave is the philosopher's work in contemplating truth.[7] It is part of the process of education. It is the work of the soul reaching up into the intelligible realm. In the allegory nothing of any consequence is said or heard when the prisoner breaks his chains and is pulled out of the cave to see the Form of the Good in all its

---

4. Martin Heidegger explains the importance for the Greeks of something being brought into view, *apophanisis*, so it can be seen for understanding and grasping (*Fundamental Concepts of Metaphysics*, 320).

5. Plato, *Republic*, 167–72.

6. John Calvin specifically says: "That human life is like smoke or shadow is not only obvious to the learned, but even ordinary folk have no proverb more commonplace than this" (Calvin, *Institutes*, 1:714).

7. Plato, *Republic*, 170.

brightness. Truth comes from seeing beyond the world of appearances to the true world of Ideas.

If you see the eternal truths, meaning you understand them, then you understand reality. Listen to Plato:

> This is how I *see* it, namely that in the intelligible world the Form of the Good is the last to be *seen*, and with difficulty; when *seen* it must be reckoned to be for all the cause of all that is right and beautiful, to have produced in the *visible* world both *light* and the *fount of light*, while in the intelligible world it is itself that which produces and controls truth and intelligence.[8]

Seeing then is central to understanding and what makes knowing truth possible for the philosopher. And this is seeing with the mind's eye.

In contrast, Judaism and Christianity are religions of the word that call believers to hear and then act. According to Kittel:

> This prevalence of hearing points to an essential feature of biblical religion. It is a religion of the Word, because it is a religion of action, of obedience to the Word. The prophet is the bearer of the Word of Yahweh which demands obedience and fulfilment. Man is not righteous as he seeks to apprehend or perceive God by way of thought and vision, but as he hears the command of God and studies to observe it. It is thus that he "seeks the Lord" (Jer 29:13).[9]

In fact, the Old Testament ties action and obedience together with God's call. Unlike the Greek view of knowledge, it is not the seeing, apprehending, understanding, and grasping truth of the armchair philosopher. It is not correct thinking; it is correct doing. Certainly, understanding is important in the Old Testament, but it is important in the way Ps 111:10 explains obedience: "The fear of the Lord is the beginning of wisdom; A good understanding have all those who do His commandments."

The prophet Micah shows how this hearing-then-doing of God's word works: "He has told you, O man, what is good; and what does the Lord require of you but to do justice, to love kindness, and to walk humbly with your God?" (Mic 6:8). In other words, Micah says now that you have heard God's word, go do it. He doesn't call for contemplating and objectifying knowledge in the mind; he calls for obedience that wills and acts.

---

8. Plato, *Republic*, 170. Emphasis added.
9. Gerhard Kittel, "ακούω," *TDNT* 1:210–25, esp. 1:218.

It follows that the Old Testament view of knowledge and knowing is broader than the Greek concept because it does not separate the mind from the body and knowing from acting. The Old Testament view commands the hearer to be a doer. Knowledge is subjective as Kierkegaard describes it. For the Greeks, knowing is an objective relationship between the knowing subject and the knowledge that inheres in the mind.

In the Old Testament, knowing is not simply an objective relationship, because an existential calling arises between the knowledge and the hearer's willing and acting. Biblical truth is objective, but you cannot eliminate the call to act by reducing it to contemplating it from without or by simply learning theology and doctrine and properly understanding biblical truth. Indeed, doctrine can become a detour. By now my readers should recognize the pagan seeing-as-understanding pattern as the way Bourgeois Christians think. But the biblical view of knowledge is different.

In the Old Testament, knowledge means knowledge of God, his acts, his promises, and his law. Knowledge makes a claim on the hearer. It is covenantal. It is not a knowledge that "objectively investigates and describes reality" like the Greek view.[10] Rather, knowledge within the covenant between God and his people makes claims on them: God blesses and demands action from his people at the same time.[11] This is clear from Deuteronomy, where God's blessings and the call to obedience go together. The covenantal relationship entails special duties, not special exemptions.[12] Or as Calvin says, we are priests in Christ to "offer ourselves and our all to God."[13]

Consequently, biblical knowledge is the knowledge of God in action, especially God's actions with men. Contrary to the Greek idea, it is not knowledge of his eternal essence; it is the knowledge of God's claim on men and his rule over the creation.[14] "Knowledge is not thought of in terms of the possession of information. It is possessed only in its exercise or actualisation."[15] King David shows the knowledge-action pattern in Ps 119. He meditates to learn the law. He learns the law to avoid the false way and to walk the faithful way. He observes the law in the sense of obeying

---

10. Bultmann, *TDNT* 1:697.

11. See generally the book of Deuteronomy. This carries over into the New Testament and the new covenant.

12. Westphal, *Suspicion & Faith*, 64.

13. Calvin, *Institutes*, 1:502.

14. Bultmann, *TDNT* 1:698.

15. Bultmann, *TDNT* 1:698.

it and applying it, not just understanding it. In fact, David is going to run the way of the law (Ps 119:27–32). This hearing-then-doing pattern continues in the New Testament.

In the New Testament, hearing is still essential, although seeing-as-understanding is important. When the prophet John the Baptist sends messengers to Jesus to ask if he is the "Expected One," Jesus says, "Go and report to John what you hear and see" (Matt 11:4). The writer of Hebrews asks, "How will we escape if we neglect so great a salvation? After it was at the first spoken through the Lord, it was confirmed to us by those who heard" (Heb 2:3). At the transfiguration: "Then a cloud formed, overshadowing them, and a voice came out of the cloud, 'This is My beloved Son, listen to Him!'" (Mark 9:7). The Bible recognizes both an external hearing and a true hearing demonstrated by acting on biblical truth. Hence, Jesus says about the parables, "He who has ears to hear, let him hear" (Mark 4:9). The parables not only teach truth; they warn against both evil action and a no-action kind of Christianity.[16]

Also in the New Testament, the message directs the hearer, and the message is "always the offering of salvation and ethical demand in one. Hearing, then, is always the reception both of grace and of the call to repentance.... There thus arises, as the crowning concept of the obedience which consists in faith and the faith which consists in obedience."[17] There is no disengaged reason and no disembodied faith described here because disengaged reason and disembodied faith have no place in the Christian life. Rather, the prevailing kind of knowing in the Bible is a hearing-then-doing, and this kind of learning benefits the believer and the covenant community because the knower uses knowledge to obey God and love neighbors.

None of this discussion, however, should lead one to conclude that seeing-as-understanding has no place in Christian teaching. The problem is when seeing-as-understanding trumps hearing-then-doing as the fundamental way of understanding the Bible, or when one fails to understand that the Bible is very much a book of duties.[18] The problem occurs when correct thought becomes more important than the neighbor and learning more important than doing. And when seeing-as-understanding holds

---

16. The parable of the sower and the parable of the ten virgins both warn against no action. See Luke 8:4–15 and Matt 25:1–13.

17. Kittel, *TDNT* 1:220.

18. One should not conclude that Greek thought never leads to action. Plato's *Republic* and Aristotle's *Politics* both show the need for action.

sway in the Cartesian consciousness, Bourgeois Christians adopt a paganized view of Christian understanding. It is an Aristotelian view.

At the end of his *Nicomachean Ethics*, Aristotle explains that the best life is the life of leisurely contemplation. "The intellect [*nous*] is the most excellent of the things in us, and the things with which the intellect is concerned are the most excellent of the things that can be known."[19] For Aristotle the human intellect is something divine, and the activity of the intellect is superior to other ethical activity.[20] And most importantly, "the person who is active in accord with the intellect, who cares for this and is in the best condition regarding it, also seems to be dearest to the gods."[21] Therein grows one pagan root of the weeds of the Cartesian consciousness and Aristotle's view that valorizes the mind. This view infests those churches that believe God is happy with them because of their theology. And of course, each denomination believes that its view of biblical truth is God's view of truth.

Thus, following the Greeks, Bourgeois Christians believe that what makes God happy with them is what is in their minds. Or, what makes them godlike is their intellect—a mind separated from the body. Yet, you know in a practical way that there is no separation. When you hit your thumb with a hammer, do you say that your mind hurts? I don't play the piano with my mind; I play it with my fingers. You can't separate your mind from your body.

But for Bourgeois Christians, sanctification means becoming more like God in their minds, and sanctification becomes the process of learning. Being like God becomes understanding God by storing biblical truth in the mind, and this makes the Christian life primarily a life of seeing, grasping, apprehending, and organizing biblical truth for insight, which paganizes Christian understanding. This is a paradox that leads to worldliness. It puts new wine into 2300-year-old wine skins—Greek thought.

On the other hand, J. I. Packer describes what it means to know God. In *Knowing God*, Packer explains that "first, *knowing God is a matter of personal dealing*, as is all direct acquaintance with personal beings. Knowing God is more than knowing about him; it is a matter of dealing with him as he opens up to you, and being dealt with by him as he takes knowledge of you."[22] As Packer further explains, "*Knowing God is a mat-*

19. Aristotle, *Nicomachean Ethics*, 224, 1177a.
20. Aristotle, *Nicomachean Ethics*, 225, 1177b.
21. Aristotle, *Nicomachean Ethics*, 229, 1179a.
22. Packer, *Knowing God*, 39. Emphasis in original.

ter of personal involvement—mind, will, and feeling." Indeed, the width of our knowledge about God is "no gauge of the depth of our knowledge of him." Furthermore, the way to gain the knowledge of God is "to commit yourself to his company and interests, and be ready to identify yourself with his concerns."[23]

The knowledge-culture dodge can smother the spirit rather than stoke the fires of action. Certainly, there is a place for this type of teaching, and even though beauty can inspire action, it often degenerates into the worldliness of the aesthetic mindset in which seeing the truth frees one from living the truth. And this leads to a key point.

Robust theology well taught does not mean robust theology well received, even when the hearers "receive it with joy," like the second-soil hearers in the parable of the sower (Matt 13:20). The Bourgeois Christian aesthete sees but does not see, and hears but does not hear, and therefore does not understand (Matt 13:13). But because many teachers and preachers don't understand the worldly influence of the aesthete's approach to knowledge, they think that because their hearers learn something or get excited about the teaching, it works, even when nothing changes in their hearers' lives. They may be alive intellectually, but they are asleep spiritually. A preacher can have a "great ministry" that excites people yet changes few lives, because their hearing is aesthetic, not existential. This is part of the age and common in evangelical churches. Yet there is an important place for the aesthetic in the church.

God's beauty is prominent in the Bible, especially in the Psalms where we find the spiritual power of beauty. The Bible urges closeness to God, the worship of God, feeling the power and glory of being a child of God, the majesty of God, and the stirring vision of God's beauty. Examples include God exalted in Ps 33, God worshipped in Ps 29, the joy of the psalmist beholding the beauty of God in Ps 27:4, and the psalmist resting in the comfort and love of God in Ps 23:1–3.

All these express emotion, joy, and endearment to God and glorify him. Indeed, these verses reflect the personal involvement that Packer describes. They express fellowship, sonship, and unity with God. Nothing that I say in this chapter diminishes the importance of this kind of biblical teaching and biblical understanding. Nothing diminishes the importance of the beauty of Christ. Rather, this chapter is about how God's beauty or the Bible's beauty is understood by the hearer. Is it the understanding, will, and emotion that glorifies God, or is it the aesthete understanding

---

23. Packer, *Knowing God*, 39. Emphasis in original.

something interesting in the Bible? The first is a spiritual power that transforms. The second is an intellectual interest driven by our aesthetic culture that deforms and deflects Christian truth.

Consequently, when preachers and teachers appeal to the aesthetic, they must beware the spiritual emptiness that beautiful knowledge can hide. Aesthetic teaching becomes paradoxical when it follows the spirit of the age that dominates the culture adrift in tastes and values. Understanding the aesthetic in this way is very important because it explains why churchgoers love good sermons and interesting Bible teaching, but the teaching makes little difference in their lives. They listen aesthetically because they are connoisseurs of sermons—a matter of taste, not conviction.

Bourgeois Christians claim to love sound preaching, but they really want interesting preaching. As a result, for many Evangelicals, preaching no longer exhorts; it only pleases or displeases because they do not hear it existentially. They don't hear God's claim on their lives. Consequently, for Bourgeois Christians the aesthetic understanding has defeated the "onward Christian soldier" attitude, and a phantom army has replaced a servant army on the battlefield of life.

Finally, this chapter on hearing-then-doing ties into the last chapter on the heart because hearing-then-doing operates in the heart. The mind is part of the heart, but just one part. The heart is what controls life and combines knowledge, will, emotions, and passions into action. On the other hand, the Bourgeois Christian view of the mind holds sway as the pagan view of seeing-as-understanding. It is about grasping and apprehending truth and then putting it into the bank account of the mind. The more knowledge you have in the account, the more you are worth to God. Unfortunately, this approach fortifies spiritual lethargy and dignifies theological correctness. But to the contrary, Psalms teaches that when the heart is enlarged, the believer runs faster (Ps 119:32).[24] Only fast feet outrun the rising tide of the age.

The next chapter describes the idea of living the truth and explains what truth is. Making Christian truth existential is the unconcealing of God's power in a Christian's life. It is the incarnate, embodied life that flows from God's power, operates in God's kingdom, and is embedded in the dirt of the world.

---

24. About this verse William S. Plumer says, "It marks great alacrity in the business of serving God" (*Psalms*, 1034).

Chapter 10 The Truth Is *Aletheia*

EVANGELICALS DO NOT UNDERSTAND truth, and rather than having a biblical view of it, they let the age control their understanding. This is not a complete misunderstanding. Rather, it is an incomplete and impoverished view of what truth is. While Evangelicals know many biblical truths, they do not know what truth means in a fundamental sense, and this failure can misdirect them in serving God.

Along with the Cartesian mind/body dualism, the pagan view of the mind versus the biblical view of the heart, and the pagan seeing-as-understanding, comes the problem of knowing the essence of truth. The truth problem shapes one's understanding of reality. Truth fundamentally engages our bodies. Jesus is an embodied person, the incarnate God-man, truth in a body. Jesus's disclosing truth by embodying it is the primary way his followers reveal Christian truth in their lives. Truth in its essence is something incarnated and embodied—something worked out in space and time. Truth is *aletheia*, and *aletheia* is action. And as I will show, understanding truth as *aletheia* solves some problems that confuse Evangelicals.

Describing truth as *aletheia* and *aletheia* as action is fundamental to the essence of truth. Foremost, the essence of truth as *aletheia* describes an uncovering and disclosing of being. This is first-order truth. Other ways of understanding truth are not wrong; they are secondary, corollary, or descriptive. They are true because they correspond to or describe what is disclosed. Moreover, truth as *aletheia* deals primarily with beings and not with ideas, and this shift away from accurate thought to spiritual being changes the goals of the Christian life. Truth as *aletheia* dissolves the mind/body dualism. Truth as correspondence and accord of subject and object can leaven the loaf and fill it with air by making knowledge, not action, what really matters.

Consequently, truth is not primarily correctness and accuracy of representations or statements. It is not primarily agreement of subject and object and not primarily something that takes place in the mind. I am not rejecting or discrediting representational truth or thinking about truth. *Representational* means a statement of truth that stands for, explains, or summarizes some other truth that arises out of action. But viewing Christian truth primarily as a collection of ideas to be learned and organized in the mind intellectualizes it, and that paganizes it. This is a problem even when the ideas are biblical.

Furthermore, making seeing-as-understanding the primary mode of truth and how one deals with it follows the pagan culture of ancient Greece. It is also a sign of the Cartesian consciousness. As with the other pagan concepts, the modern view of truth raises spiritual hurdles to stymie Evangelicals in the race that God calls them to run with endurance (Heb 12:1). And because Bourgeois Christians understand truth as a system of propositions to be learned, they lumber along the byways of spiritual lethargy or theological correctness. But what truth as *aletheia* means requires careful study.

In *Parmenides* Martin Heidegger describes this pre-Socratic philosopher's view of truth as *aletheia*. He argues that the West has lost the primordial essence of truth as unconcealedness and that for two millennia the concept of truth has degenerated. His argument is long and complex, and I borrow a few of his ideas and then part company with him to offer my own view of *aletheia* and embodiment. In fact, understanding truth as *aletheia* works better in a biblical context than it does for Heidegger because *aletheia* is fundamental to biblical truth and essential for Christian ethics.

First, remember for Heidegger and for my analysis, *aletheia* deals primarily with beings, not with statements, nor with believing statements. Heidegger explains that "for the Greeks, and still in Aristotle, *aletheia* is a character of beings and not a characteristic of the perceiving of beings and of assertions about them."[1] For example, it is true that Jesus is God incarnate. But the statement is not the reality. It describes reality. In the primary sense, Jesus is *aletheia* in the flesh. And John 1:14 proclaims this ultimate revealing of truth—the unconcealing of God: "And the Word became flesh, and dwelt among us, and we saw His glory, glory as of the only begotten

---

1. Heidegger, *Parmenides*, 34.

from the Father, full of grace and truth." Although the statement is true, it is the action or the event of disclosure itself that is the *aletheia* of Christ. The event, the act, makes the statement true. Jesus came to earth as a man, not as a Bible verse. Jesus became flesh. A statement can never become flesh. As Kittel explains, the incarnation is not about a concept or, to use another word, a doctrine. To think of it in this way is to hopelessly distort it.[2] And the idea of truth has been distorted in the modern age.

Heidegger says the essence of truth in the modern age is no longer unconcealedness; it is accuracy of understanding, correctness of statement, and agreement of subject and object. Plato promoted this view, and it replaced the understanding of truth as unconcealment and disclosure of being.[3] For example, Atlanta is the capital of Georgia, and George Washington was America's first president. Both statements are accurate, and if we agree with them in our minds, then we have truth according to modern understanding.

But what truth problem does paganism smuggle into the Christian camp? Or more importantly, what does it smuggle out? In Heidegger's understanding of modern metaphysics, it subverts the question of being because the question of thinking and the focus on consciousness has replaced the question of what it means to be. Heidegger says the question of being has been lost in history.

Heidegger begins his history of truth as unconcealedness by showing that the pre-Socratic philosopher Parmenides uses the word *aletheia* for truth.[4] The word *aletheia* begins with the *a* (alpha) of the Greek alpha privativum, which indicates a taking away or cancelling. We recognize the alpha privativum in words like "atheist" and "agnostic." The remainder of the word *aletheia* means covering or concealing, specifically the concealing of being, and that Greek word is *lethe*. Therefore, the literal translation of *aletheia* means unconcealedness, disclosure, or unhiddenness.

---

2. Gerhard Kittel, "λέγω," *TDNT* 4:69–136, esp. 4:125. "It is to be noted however—and this is of absolutely decisive importance—that these statements do not rest on a concept of the 'Word.' If they are understood conceptually, they are wholly and hopelessly distorted. They arise, and derive their life, only from the event which is given in the person of Jesus. At the head of the train of thought sketched by the term *logos* there stands, not a concept, but the event which has taken place, and in which God declares Himself, causing His Word to be enacted."

3. See generally Heidegger, "Plato's Doctrine of Truth."

4. Heidegger, *Parmenides*, 11.

Heidegger says, however, that simply translating the Greek word into English does not explain the ancient world understanding of truth as unconcealedness. In other words, what was it about the ancient Greek world that caused Parmenides to believe that truth is fundamentally concealed in everyday life?

If the ancient Greek philosophers understood truth as *aletheia*, meaning unconcealedness, then they believed that reality was concealed in some way. False appearances cover over the true being of beings, and mere opinions hide truth. Consequently, one must overcome the concealedness of beings to have truth. The essence of truth is taking away or annihilating concealedness, so truth stands in opposition to and struggles against concealedness.[5]

In the modern view, the opposite of what is true is what is false or incorrect. For our age, what is false is the opposite of truth understood as correctness or accuracy. This falseness is in a person's mind or in a statement or both. And although Heidegger does not disagree with this view of truth, nor do I, truth as *aletheia* is more fundamental, and he tells us more about its characteristics.

Heidegger describes three elements of the primordial essence of truth as *aletheia*. First, concealedness permeates primordial truth. Truth is hidden. From its foundation, concealedness is fundamental to reality. Second, one must wrench truth from concealedness, so truth battles concealedness. And third, concealedness opposes truth as *aletheia* in all of life.[6] Below, I show how these three elements of *aletheia* fit Jesus's redemptive work. But first, look at two examples of how Plato exposes concealedness.

Plato uses the dialectical method in his dialogues to overcome and stand against concealedness. The *Euthyphro* offers a good example of overcoming and standing against. In that dialogue Socrates cross-examines a self-proclaimed religious expert to expose his ignorance and his false practices because Euthyphro's appearance and speech cover up his ignorance and impiety. Socrates, therefore, "unconceals" Euthyphro's impious being. He also exposes Euthyphro's false religious ideas, and that was part of Socrates's unconcealing of Euthyphro's false being. What does false mean here?

The Greek idea of false is not concealment. Rather it is *pseudos*, and *pseudos* is a dissembling, and dissembling is a kind of obstructing or

---

5. Heidegger, *Parmenides*, 16.
6. Heidegger, *Parmenides*, 26.

disguising.[7] It is an appearance, but a false appearance that conceals. Think back to Plato's allegory of the cave and the shadows that the captors cast on the wall. The prisoners believe that these shadows, these appearances, are reality; yet they are deceived. The shadows do reveal something, but they do not reveal reality. Indeed, the captors hide reality from the prisoners by staging false appearances of beings.

Remember that *pseudos* as falseness and *aletheia* as truth are primarily characteristics of beings, not statements.[8] Euthyphro made false statements, but his fundamental problem was a problem of being. His being was false because of the way he lived. The transition then from truth as unconcealedness (*aletheia*) to the modern view of truth as correctness and accuracy is not simply a change in the understanding of the essence of truth. Something else has changed.

The modern view of truth changes the locus of truth—where and how truth primarily operates. In the modern view of subjectivity as Descartes initiated it, truth is no longer primarily in the existence of beings. It is now something found in statements and propositions about beings mediated by the human mind.[9] It operates primarily in our consciousness as psychological events for Descartes and for Bourgeois Christians.

Furthermore, with the transition to truth as the accuracy of statements in the mind, the essence of the mind's job becomes adjusting to what is correct and accurate.[10] The goal becomes having the right truth in one's consciousness, rather than in the heart biblically understood. But because truth is *aletheia*, it is existential—involving your total existence, not primarily psychological. And as Heidegger explains, what is lost is the understanding that "truth ultimately demands the engagement of man as a whole."[11]

This means truth is a matter of the heart that engages the whole person. Truth is embodied and then revealed. But in the modern view of truth that joins its locus and operation primarily in consciousness, we are back to the Bourgeois Christians' efforts to furnish their minds with correct ideas, while embodying those ideas becomes secondary, a kind of parenthesis or footnote on spirituality. So how does the Bible use the word *aletheia*?

7. Heidegger, *Parmenides*, 33.
8. Heidegger, *Parmenides*, 34.
9. Heidegger, *Parmenides*, 50.
10. Heidegger, *Parmenides*, 50.
11. Heidegger, *Fundamental Concepts of Metaphysics*, 29.

The first question for Christians is whether *aletheia* is translated as truth in the New Testament. According to the *New American Standard Exhaustive Concordance of the Bible*, truth is used approximately one hundred times in the New Testament. *Aletheia* is the Greek word translated as "truth" every time except four in the NASB. Three of those four are derivatives of *aletheia*.[12] Consequently, we routinely find *aletheia* translated as "truth" in the Bible.

It helps to interpret some important biblical passages by using *aletheia* understood as an unconcealing. I do not contend, however, that this is the only way that the word "truth" is used or understood in the New Testament, but unconcealing is fundamental to the truth of these verses.

The incarnation described in John 1:14 unconceals God. Jesus's becoming flesh and dwelling as flesh are essential to understanding this verse. Christ's coming is a revealing, a revealing of what had been prophesied but hidden in the Old Testament. The incarnation allowed the world to see God because Jesus is God and explains God with more than words (John 1:18). Jesus's incarnation is the revealing of "the mystery, which was kept secret since the world began" (Rom 16:25). Moreover, Jesus did not take on a body just so he could die on the cross. His life reveals God, and as he says, "He who has seen Me has seen the Father" (John 14:9). Jesus calls himself the Light of the world (John 9:5). Light discloses. Light reveals the concealed.

The incarnation was the greatest unconcealing, the greatest disclosing of all time. As Heb 1:3 teaches: "[Jesus] is the radiance of His glory and the exact representation of His nature," referring to God. Indeed, the apostle Paul says that Jesus is the image of God (2 Cor 4:4). And the "full of grace and truth" in John 1:14 does not mean simply full of theological truths; it describes both the fullness of God's being and God's love shown in God's action.

Likewise, in John 14:6 Jesus says, "I am the way and the [*aletheia*] and the life." Jesus embodies God, who is spirit and has no body. Jesus is truth in a body. William Hendriksen, a prominent Dutch Calvinist, explains that "Jesus is the very embodiment of the truth. He is the truth in person. As such he is the final reality in contrast with the shadows which preceded him."[13] Notice the words "embodiment" and "shadows." His embodiment overcomes the shadows of concealment (Col 2:17).[14] The shadows of the

---

12. Thomas, *Concordance*, 1629.
13. Hendriksen, *Gospel According to John*, 268.
14. "Things which are a mere shadow of what is to come; but the substance belongs

Old Testament, commonly called types, and his coming that the prophets foretold, reveal truth about him and his work by his bodily appearance.

Hendriksen further says about John 14:6: "But in the present context the term *the truth* seems to have a different shade of meaning. It is that which stands over against the lie. Jesus is the truth because He is *the dependable source of redemptive revelation*."[15] Jesus reveals God and God's redemptive purpose. He also stands against the darkness of lies.

Jesus personifies truth as *aletheia* as Heidegger describes it. First, being an example is essential to Jesus's work. Because he embodies God, he is not only Savior and Lord; he reveals life in a body as an example of love. After washing his disciples' feet, Jesus says, "For I gave you an example that you also should do as I did to you" (John 13:15). The point is not to wash people's feet but to embody service and love. The apostle Peter similarly says, "For you have been called for this purpose, since Christ also suffered for you, leaving you an example for you to follow in His steps" (1 Pet 2:21). Paul also exhorts believers to "in all things show yourself to be an example of good deeds" (Titus 2:7). So the incarnation was an event in time that gave Jesus's followers the example of what *aletheia* is and how to embody it.

In this same vein, the apostle Luke describes his Gospel's purpose as compiling "an account of the things accomplished among us" (Luke 1:1). He is referring to what Jesus did while on earth, which covers more than his teaching. When John the Baptist's disciples came to ask Jesus if he is the Christ, Jesus does not answer by saying yes or by making claims about himself. He points to his deeds. He says: "Go and report to John what you have seen and heard: the blind receive sight, the lame walk, the lepers are cleansed, and the deaf hear, the dead are raised up, the poor have the gospel preached to them" (Luke 7:22). Jesus lived an action life—a showing life, a revealing life.

Jesus's followers should live revealing lives. He makes his followers' duties clear. In Matt 5:14–16, Jesus describes one way of unconcealing Christian being:

> You are the light of the world. A city set on a hill cannot be hidden; nor does anyone light a lamp and put it under a basket, but on the lampstand, and it gives light to all who are in the house. Let your light shine before men in such a way that they may see your good works, and glorify your Father who is in heaven.

---

to Christ."

15. Hendriksen, *Gospel According to John*, 268. Emphasis in original.

This is a vivid metaphor for disclosing the power of God in a believer's life. This revealing is an unconcealing. As Hendriksen explains about this verse: "The followers of Christ must be both *visible* and *radiant*."[16]

Likewise, Christians are the temple of God (2 Cor 6:16). God dwells within them. About this verse, Charles Hodge explains that the believer's soul "is said to be full of God when its inward state, its affections and acts, are determined and controlled by him, so as to be a constant manifestation of the divine presence."[17] Manifesting the divine presence is embodying the divine presence. And like a temple, the Christian's life should be open in the public square for all to see.

Sometimes the unfaithful are unconcealed to show their lawlessness. As the apostle John says: "They went out from us, but they were not really of us; for if they had been of us, they would have remained with us; but they went out, so that it would be shown that they all are not of us" (1 John 2:19). Also, Demas deserted Paul because of his love for the world, and Demas's leaving showed his love for the world and not for Christ (2 Tim 4:10).

Hebrews 12:1 describes the Christian life as a race run before "so great a cloud of witnesses." The imagery is Greek, like Olympic racers in a stadium filled with spectators. These spectators are believers from the past who have faithfully served God and inherited eternal life. Their good works, which Heb 11 describes, are offered as examples to exhort believers running the race of faith. In this relay race for eternity, they have passed their batons to the next generation of believers. And as nineteenth-century Calvinist commentator John Brown explains, "The whole of Christian duty is represented as a race—a race set before them, which they must run, and 'run with patience.' The principal ideas suggested by this figurative view of Christian duty are the following: It is active, laborious, regulated, progressive, persevering exertion."[18] Or as Martin Luther says: "We must never stand still in seeking after God."[19] Because it is a race before spectators, it is for all to see, and it discloses God's power in believers' lives. All believers are on God's track team.

Similarly, many verses describe the believer's duty to bear fruit. A tree's fruit defines the tree and its usefulness. The apple hangs from the limb and shows that the tree is an apple tree. The fruit is the unconcealing of what

---

16. Hendriksen, *Gospel According to Matthew*, 285. Emphasis in original.
17. Hodge, *Commentary on Corinthians*, 547.
18. Brown, *Hebrews*, 604.
19. Luther, *Commentary on Romans*, 71.

the tree is, and a fruit tree that does not bear fruit is worthless. Jesus makes clear the believer's duty to bear fruit. In John 15:16, Jesus says: "You did not choose me but I chose you, and appointed you that you would go and bear fruit, and that your fruit would remain."

Bearing fruit is an unconcealing like letting your light shine before men. Jesus also says that "each tree is known by its own fruit" (Luke 6:44). The good man, the believer, brings forth good fruit, and the evil man brings forth bad fruit (Luke 6:45).[20] Bourgeois Christians believe that Jesus saves them to go to heaven. Paul tells them that Jesus saves them to bear fruit (Rom 7:4).[21]

Likewise, Jas 2:17 says, "Even so faith, if it has no works, is dead, being by itself." Works is like fruit in the previous verses. Substituting fruit for works in this verse makes the same point: "Even so faith, if it has no fruit is dead, being by itself." The apostle James continues in 2:24: "You see that man is justified by works and not by faith alone." So when truth is *aletheia*, an unconcealing and disclosing of being when it embodies love, then the importance of works is obvious, not some mystery.[22] Works don't save, but they are necessary for working out one's salvation, which, according to the apostle Paul, is done with fear and trembling (Phil 2:12). And as Calvin says, it is a matter of sequence, not salvation.[23] The faith/works "mystery" is one of the specious theological problems in contemporary Evangelicalism. The apostles John, Paul, Peter, and James all emphasize works to one degree or another, and it is no mystery when you understand truth as *aletheia*.

This view of truth also explains religious hypocrisy. Hypocrites, specifically the Pharisees, flaunted religious appearances. They exemplify *pseudos*, and *pseudos* is dissembling and opposes *aletheia*. They were whitewashed tombs (Matt 23:27). Hypocrites offer an appearance of righteousness, but it is a false appearance, a dissembling. What hypocrites say or how they act may look good and sound good, but hypocrites do not have the being of truth because they don't embody truth.

---

20. "The good man out of the good treasure of his heart brings forth what is good; and the evil man out of the evil treasure brings forth what is evil; for his mouth speaks from that which fills his heart."

21. "Therefore, my brethren, you also were made to die to the Law through the body of Christ, so that you might be joined to another, to Him who was raised from the dead, in order that we might bear fruit for God."

22. As John Calvin explains: "The same Spirit teaches through James that the faith both of Abraham and of ourselves consists in works, not only in faith" (*Institutes*, 1:814).

23. Calvin, *Institutes*, 1:821.

For example, the Pharisees tithed their herbs but neglected what God most desired: justice, mercy, and faithfulness (Matt 23:23). Justice and mercy involve relationships, and faithfulness is showing love in those relationships. The Pharisees concealed God's truth in their religious practices and led others astray.

How does Phariseeism manifest itself in Evangelicalism? That the Pharisees are dead does not mean that Phariseeism is dead. It thrives as Bourgeois Christianity in evangelical churches, but it is unnoticed. The Pharisees devised a religion that they could keep and, at the same time, look good doing it. Bourgeois Christians have the knowledge culture to make them look good. But this mission drift takes Christians out of the spiritual war zone and nestles them in the cultural comfort zone. They don't need spiritual armor for this duty. But this kind of learning is an "always learning and never able to come to the knowledge of the truth"—that is, that the truth is *aletheia* (2 Tim 3:7).

Understanding the essence of truth is fundamental in determining whether one is on the back road of Bourgeois Christianity or on the freeway of heart-driven spirituality. As twentieth-century philosopher Hannah Arendt explains: "For, unlike the judgment of the intellect which precedes action, and unlike the command of the will which initiates it, the inspiring principle becomes fully manifest only in the performing act itself."[24] The inspiring principle is Jesus, and he inspires love by his example. Love is a verb, and so is faith. And if you doubt that faith is a verb, look at the heroes of Heb 11 and Abraham's life.

Furthermore, regarding the Christian's duty to embody and reveal truth, what is usually missed, yet is so obvious, is that God created people with bodies. For the Christian, the body is not some clumsy limb that stumbles behind the Cartesian *cogito*. That Christians have bodies stands against the Cartesian mind/body dualism with its emphasis on the mind that renders the body secondary. The body is a fundamental argument against Bourgeois Christianity and its mind-centered approach to being a Christian. Jesus had a bodily resurrection. Believers get a new body at the end of the age. *Aletheia* operates through the body.

Without *aletheia*'s unconcealment, without the individual's will applying truth, truth becomes simply an abstraction: theoretical, hypothetical, general, or a series of psychological events mediated by the mind. But as the philosopher Hegel observes: "The distinction between thought and will is simply that between theoretical and practical attitudes. But they are not

---

24. Arendt, *Between Past and Future*, 151.

two separate faculties; on the contrary, the will is a particular way of thinking—thinking translating itself into existence, thinking as the drive to give itself existence."[25] Christian truth calls forth the drive to give itself existence in believers' lives and empowers them to act through the Spirit.

In summary, Jesus, who is God, is truth and not just because he knows truth, speaks truth, or teaches truth. He embodies truth. His life is life's essence. His death is the quintessence of truth that sends a simple message of service and sacrifice. His teaching would be worthless without his bodily suffering, death, and resurrection. And because God is truth, truth is power translated into action, and power without action is meaningless.

God's power converts Christians to the truth; they learn truth to embody it in relationships. Jewish philosopher Martin Buber, responding to the damage that the Cartesian mindset has wreaked in the modern age, explains it well: "The strongest and deepest actuality is to be found where everything enters into activity—the whole human being, without reserve, and the all-embracing god; the unified I and the boundless You."[26] He is talking about the relationship between the individual and God that produces action. As a Jew, Buber understood the Hebrew Bible well. God is always in action in the Old Testament. Jesus is always in action in the New Testament.

Finally, what Kierkegaard says about the church in Denmark applies to Bourgeois Christians:

> I do not think that without exaggeration one can say that Christianity in our time has been completely abolished. No, Christianity still exists and in its truth, but as a *teaching*, as *doctrine*. What has been abolished and forgotten (and this can be said without exaggeration), however, is being a Christian, what it means to be a Christian; or what has been lost, what seems to exist no longer, is the ideal picture of being a Christian.[27]

British historian G. R. Cragg identified the year when this began for the Calvinists in England. After the Restoration of 1660 and the king's return, "Calvinism became more of an abstract Scriptural dogmatism."[28] That is where the neo-Calvinists are today. How do theological systems contribute to this problem? That is the topic of the next chapter.

25. Hegel, *Philosophy of Right*, 35.
26. Buber, *I and Thou*, 137.
27. Kierkegaard, *Point of View*, 129–30. Emphasis in original.
28. Cragg, *From Puritanism*, 36. Cragg argues that Puritanism lost its cultural and political power abruptly after the Restoration.

Chapter 11 **Problems with a System —Even a Good One**

I AM ANSWERING THE question asked in the introduction about why churches with biblical preaching, church discipline, and sacramental worship produce Bourgeois Christians. This chapter shows how sound theological systems can breed the Cartesian consciousness of Bourgeois Christianity.

Theological systems influence church teaching and practices. Paradoxically, a system of biblical truth can promote Bourgeois Christian intellectualism and its existential barrenness. Too much emphasis on teaching and learning is one trait of a Christian knowledge culture. Indeed, theological systems, those anchors against the storms of heresy and guides for church members, can stifle the embodied Christian life by distracting rather than by inspiring believers. "Faith without works is dead," says James. The intellectualist churches alter that a little: "Faith without words is dead." This is a paradox. The thin cloth of theology can hide the existential thickness of the Christian life.

This chapter, however, does not contest the truths offered in any theological system. The question is not "What does this theological system do for me?" Others have answered this question well. Rather, recognizing the influences and the mind/body dualism of the age, I ask, "What can a theological system do *to* me?" Or "How can a theological system hinder rather than enhance serving God and neighbor?"[1]

---

1. One should not conclude from this chapter that I believe that Evangelicals should reject doctrine. Indeed, it is likely that the lack of interest in doctrine is a more serious problem among Evangelicals than what I am describing. In fact, an Evangelical who rejects a systematic understanding of Scriptures to rely on their feelings is the next-door neighbor to a liberal theologian. But as explained in the introduction, this book shows

Although my method is out of the mainstream, my message is not. As Os Guinness explains, "Thus even as Christians we are prone toward turning faith in God into a system of thought about God. In so doing we remove all mystery, tie up all the loose ends with our human logic, and finally reduce even Christ to being a mere part of our system of ideas."[2] This is human reason in action, or rationality in action. This chapter explains how what Os Guinness describes creates Bourgeois Christians and the pagan power of reason and Western rationalism that goes back to Plato.

Misguided rationality, or the misuse of reason, involves the misuse of the powers of abstraction and organization. It simplifies biblical concepts and presents a conceptual view of biblical truth, which can lead to an impoverished view.[3] Reason synthesizes, organizes, and conceptualizes, the kinds of activities that many Calvinists and dispensationalists do well in ordering biblical principles. But this kind of thinking began with the ancient Greeks, and many Western theologians and philosophers have followed it for 2500 years. It overemphasizes the importance of the mind as a container for or developer of ideas. It focuses on abstractions at the expense of personal connections.

Bourgeois Christians are not continental rationalists like Descartes, Spinoza, and Leibniz, who taught that truth comes from the mind. These philosophers valorized the mind, thinking, and system building, and some Evangelicals do as well. The pattern or method is the problem, and in some denominations theological systems are very important and very influential.

What is a theological system? A system is a statement of theological or doctrinal beliefs that interpret biblical truth. They represent biblical truth. These systems are written down, published, and understood by church members as a summary of truth. Consequently, they are representational and not within the special category of biblical truth because they are not inspired. For some denominations, their doctrinal system is the touchstone of biblical authority. The Presbyterians' Westminster Confession of Faith, the Anglicans' Thirty-Nine Articles, and the Lutherans' Augsburg Confession are examples of theological systems.

A system also includes books and articles written by pastors, professors, and theologians, especially if they address denominational distinctives.

---

the problems that are difficult to detect, and therefore have an insidious effect on Christian spirituality.

2. Guinness, *Fit Bodies Fat Minds*, 144.

3. Jacobi, *Main Philosophical Writings*, 19.

Systems include books on infant baptism or the doctrine of predestination. Or more broadly, Reformed theology and Arminian theology are systems that offer opposing views on certain biblical texts.

Furthermore, systems are historical documents that address the theological controversies of the age, and they are important. (Nothing stated here says that such documents are unhelpful or unhealthy when properly understood.) For example, the Nicene Creed was written in AD 325 as a statement of Christian orthodoxy to oppose the heresies of the day. And although Evangelicals believe that biblical truth does not change, cultural applications and cultural interpretations of biblical truth do change. So biblical truth always requires a here-and-now application, which is existential and embedded. The here-and-now is the eternal present of God's kingdom.

A system has both a biblical focus and an historical context. It is easy to miss, however, that a theological system has at least two historical contexts: the historical and theological context of the age in which it was written and the here-and-now culture of the contemporary church. In 1536 John Calvin wrote his *Institutes of the Christian Religion* in which he bitterly attacked the Catholic Church because he thought it was corrupt and heretical.[4] His historical context was the social and religious upheaval of the Reformation and the birth-to-death power the pope wielded over the lives of many sixteenth-century Europeans.

What about in the twenty-first century? The Catholic Church has lost its political power, and the Reformation ended centuries ago. We live in a deeply secularized twenty-first century that is different from the religious epoch of sixteenth- and seventeenth-century Europe. Different cultures and different ages have different issues and theological problems. Indeed, as shown in the last chapter, the secular, historical, and metaphysical view of what truth is can change how Christians understand biblical truth and what Christian spirituality demands.

For example, Calvin emphasized the important doctrine of justification by faith but not solely because he thought it was sound theology. He knew that at the Council of Trent the Catholic Church had condemned justification by faith alone.[5] He believed the mercy and grace of God that *sola fide* demonstrated could free people from the "concoctions" of

---

4. References to Calvin's *Institutes* come from a translation of the 1559 edition.

5. Calvin, *Institutes*, 1:748n35. (Calvin's *Institutes* went through many additions, including several after the Council of Trent.)

popish theologians.[6] It would also free them from Catholic cultural and political power.

Likewise, Luther emphasized grace and faith because the Catholic Church emphasized works, which included the corrupt practice of selling indulgences.[7] He also embraced them because of his own frustration with working for his salvation. Today, on the other hand, we live in an era of evangelical hyper-grace. It is the era of justification without sanctification.[8] It is the era of decisional regeneration in which "will" and "work" are dirty words, and the relationship between works and grace is some "deep mystery." So historical contexts are important for understanding the origin and influence of theological systems and their emphases.

Systems, however, are not simply historical. Calvin's and Luther's attacks on Catholicism show something fundamental about them. Theological systems are partisan. They take sides on theological issues. Presbyterians vie with Baptists over infant baptism, and Reformed writers dispute with Arminians. But beyond organizing and presenting biblical truth, these systems send a message, and that message is that "our truth is better than your truth." Or, more directly stated, "Our theology is correct, and yours is wrong."[9] This message divides God's children into different camps within God's kingdom, and sometimes the carnage occurs within the same denomination.[10] Evangelicals are like the early church that Paul criticized in 1 Corinthians because of their division: "I am of Paul," and "I am of Apollos," and "I am of Christ" (1 Cor 1:12). Except in our day it is "I am of Calvin," "I am of Arminius," or "I am of Dallas."

This partisanship leads to something difficult to see. Biblical truth becomes like a commodity—we have the genuine article, and yours is ersatz. And like a commodity, because we have the genuine article and yours is a

---

6. Calvin, *Institutes*, 1:745.

7. Luther, *Table Talk*, 505: "Because love grows by works of love, man thereby becomes better. Man does not, however, become better by means of indulgencies but is merely freed from penalties." Parenthetically, note what Luther says about love.

8. As Calvin explains: "Christ justifies no one whom he does not at the same time sanctify" (*Institutes*, 1:798).

9. Professor Wells says that the marketing impulse in some evangelical churches has turned the gospel into a product. "The gospel, understood as a product, loses its depth and cost. This happens so that its appeal and salability can be elevated, but along the way Christianity becomes flat, empty, and banal" (*Courage to Be Protestant*, 213). This is one of the reasons I say that biblical truth has been turned into a commodity.

10. See Frame, "Machen's Warrior Children."

fake, we are special. We drive the Mercedes of theology while you drive an old pickup truck. Too often this works out as "I'm a better Christian because I believe this system and you don't." Or, "If you believe this system, you will be a better Christian." Right knowledge then is the key. But these "true believers" can't see the weaknesses in their own traditions. They relax in an "I'm okay and you're okay because our doctrine is okay" attitude.

Furthermore, these systems offer discrete bits of theological truth that fit within a larger system. They come in a package of truths. But because theological and doctrinal truths are representational truths, they are necessarily biblical abstractions. They are products of human reason applied to Scripture, so they are rationalizations of biblical truth set down, organized, classified, and prioritized into a system of doctrine.[11] And as Os Guinness says, they are the product of man's logic. Doctrine becomes the external representation of the commands and acts of God. In other words, these doctrines are abstracted from the Bible.

The Westminster Confession of Faith is a good example of this abstracting process because it summarizes various doctrines in the text and then footnotes the verses supporting the summaries. It applies man's logic to interpret Scripture to bring coherence to different verses. Moreover, the truths are classified according to topics, numbered, and neatly arranged. Because systems interpret, distill, and summarize Bible verses, they are representational truth. Therefore, they are not within that special category of inspired truth found only in the Old and New Testaments. Consequently, without recognizing it, one theological camp is telling the other camp that our theological abstractions are better than yours.

Pagan rationality hidden in evangelical churches leads to a theological sideshow replacing the main event of serving. Bourgeois Christians "know" the truths, but they do not abide in them.[12] Although they may abound in knowledge, they are not following Paul's call to "abound in this gracious work [generosity] also" (2 Cor 8:7). Consequently, the neighbor is the orphan of Bourgeois Christian intellectualism and prayer its first casualty, because prayer is a spiritual exercise, not a learning opportunity.

The neighbor stops being a person and is thematized and thereby becomes a point of doctrine to be learned. Alas, it seems that the more you

---

11. See, for example, Herman Bavinck classifying the attributes of God (*Doctrine of God*, 113–251).

12. For example, John 15:10: "If ye keep my commandments, ye shall abide in my love; even as I have kept my Father's commandments, and abide in his love" (KJV).

know, the less you understand—another paradox. Bourgeois Christians become so doctrinally minded that they are of no neighborly good. Their lives are inward, self-focused, mind centered, leading to a kind of existential cul-de-sac, all consistent with the democratic culture of the age. And as Paul says, they "are looking at things as they are outwardly" (2 Cor 10:7).

But this kind of doctrinal thinking is unsituated thought.[13] Theological systems are not relational, and the Cartesian consciousness is the view from nowhere. But Christian truth is never isolated from relationships. It is always positional, acting in space, time, and history with people. Biblical understanding is relational, and that makes understanding a verb, an action verb. God's action is never isolated from relationships, if for no other reason than that the Christian God is a triune God.

This intellectualist mentality reverts to Descartes's mind/body dualism, and being a Christian reverts to thinking about being a Christian.[14] The essence of Christian spirituality, however, is not found in theological abstractions held in the consciousness of the Christian's mind. God calls his children to play their parts in his vast symphony orchestra of love. God does not call them to be musicologists. And this raises the question of what a belief is.

For Bourgeois Christians, a belief is a biblical truth understood and accepted in the mind. For example, it is accepting, believing, and continuing to believe that Jesus is the Son of God. This is intellectual assent. Philosopher José Ortega y Gasset describes belief in a better way than intellectual assent. "A belief is not merely an idea that is thought, it is an idea in which one also believes. And believing is not an operation of the intellectual mechanism, but a function of the living being as such, the function of guiding his conduct, his performance of his task."[15] Guiding and performing are the existential side of Christianity. But there is no existential side to the mere intellectual assent of the Bourgeois knowledge culture.

The knowledge culture dims duty and ends in distracting from God's kingdom goals. Knowing that Jesus is the Second Person of the Trinity in no way ensures that this belief leads to action. Furthermore, theological systems can promote the idea that some Calvinists have that God is happier with them than he is with Arminians because Calvinists have better theology. Or

---

13. This idea comes from Merleau-Ponty, *Phenomenology of Perception*, 108. Of course, the context is quite different.

14. Merleau-Ponty, *Phenomenology of Perception*, 432.

15. Ortega, *History as a System*, 167.

as one Calvinist said years ago, "The Arminians are saved, but they live on the other side of the tracks." This is sad. That biblical truth must compete with both cultural truth and denominational truth is also sad.

Truth can become shibboleths or passwords, and shibboleths are like secret fraternity handshakes—they mean nothing; they just identify you as a member of the group. They are passwords that give the appearance of spirituality. As Mark Noll explains about nineteenth-century Evangelicals, "Habits of patient study were far less well exercised than habits of quick quotation."[16] That practice is still common today—biblespeak or godtalk.

Moreover, the system conveys the idea that these truths are objective and hence separate from the believer, but truth is never separated from life. There is no sanctification without people to sanctify. There is no regeneration without hearts to regenerate. Truth is always there to wrestle with or ignore, to embrace or deny in the chaos of life. And objectifying Christian truth in this chapter means "grasping the matter studied as something quite independent of us."[17] Christian aesthetes do this. They find sermons or Christian books interesting, but they lack inwardness of spirit. And as Kierkegaard notes, "Indeed it would seem very strange that Christianity should have come into the world merely to receive an explanation."[18]

So being a Christian requires more than comprehending Christian truth. Theological correctness can conceal spiritual poverty, and doctrinal systems become like political ideologies. Furthermore, this partisanship of ideas, this denominational patriotism, conceals truth. Here we find another paradox: these systems are like religious political ideologies. What can we learn about theological systems by understanding political ideologies?

Michael Oakeshott, former professor of political science at the London School of Economics, wrote a book about political ideologies called *"Rationalism in Politics" and Other Essays*. Oakeshott was a leading conservative political theorist in twentieth-century Britain. Many of his ideas about political ideologies apply to theological systems, and like theological systems, political ideologies are historical, partisan, and selective about ideas. They generate abstractions, like the "liberty, equality, and fraternity" of the French Revolution. And ideologists establish what Oakeshott calls "vocabularies of belief."[19]

16. Noll, *Scandal of the Evangelical Mind*, 107.
17. Taylor, *Secular Age*, 746.
18. Kierkegaard, *Kierkegaard's Concluding Unscientific Postscript*, 191.
19. Oakeshott, *Rationalism in Politics*, 77.

Theologians do the same, and these doctrinal vocabularies shape their followers' views about being a Christian. Indeed, teaching is one of the main purposes of theological systems. My concern, however, is with the unintended consequences systems create with vocabularies of belief. For example, Oakeshott explains that these ideological vocabularies direct and control the understanding and actions of followers. They "invite political discourse to take certain directions and to reach certain conclusions."[20] By merely pointing in a certain direction, it becomes more difficult to look or think in another direction.[21]

Also, Oakeshott describes ideology as "an invitation to interpret political situations and to think about what is desirable and undesirable in a certain manner, and an invitation to consider some consequences of political decisions and actions to be more important than others."[22] For example, Marxism teaches that capitalism oppresses the proletariat. Classical liberalism celebrates pluralism and individualism. But what important aspects of life do they neglect?

Theological systems work in the same way because they determine not only what is theologically correct, that is, what one should believe, but also what the Christian life requires. They say what is important, which, at the same time, decides what is not important. If pastors emphasize doctrine, if teaching is the church's main goal, they emphasize learning. With every emphasis comes a de-emphasis. And if you emphasize learning too much, you produce the knowledge culture, which is an unintended but predictable result.

Thus, theological systems identify what language to use to talk about denominational priorities. The TULIP acrostic is fundamental for Calvinists. The premillennial, pre-tribulation view of the apocalypse deeply influences dispensationalists; and it is striking how often they talk about the end-times and how rarely Presbyterians do. But they argue over words. And, as philosopher Stanley Rosen explains, excessive words without deeds lead to ideologies, or in the case of the church, theological knowledge cultures lead to insight but no fight for God's kingdom.[23] Theological partisanship often ends in ethical poverty amid theological riches.

20. Oakeshott, *Rationalism in Politics*, 77.
21. Oakeshott, *Rationalism in Politics*, 74–75.
22. Oakeshott, *Rationalism in Politics*, 74.
23. Rosen, *Nihilism*, 219. Of course, denominational intellectualism causes many theological fights.

How one decides what is important in the Scriptures and what one reads into the Scriptures have a powerful control over a believer's understanding of what it means to be a Christian. Theological abstractions are both selective and directive—they select what biblical truths to emphasize and direct believers into ways of thinking. Also, like ideologies, systems take on a halo and call for allegiance, and those devoted to the system are the true believers. Hence, words have controlling effects, but they can control in the wrong direction—the broad way.

Hans-Georg Gadamer, the twentieth-century German philosopher known for his work in hermeneutics, explains one aspect of knowledge control in this way: "A person who is trying to understand a text is always projecting. He projects a meaning for the text as a whole as soon as some initial meaning emerges in the text. Again, the initial meaning emerges only because he is reading the text with particular expectations in regard to a certain meaning."[24] Theological systems create expectations for reading the Bible. In fact, one of the main purposes of theological systems is to tell their followers how to understand what certain verses mean. Consequently, there is a Reformed reading of a biblical text based on the theological priorities of Reformed thinkers and a different Arminian reading of the same text. They cannot both be right. (It certainly is possible, however, that they are both wrong, since "for now we see in a mirror dimly" [1 Cor 13:12].)[25] How do these different interpretations arise?

They arise because the Calvinist and the Arminian are reading the text and projecting their theological priorities onto it. They have decided beforehand, so to speak, what a Bible verse means, and that meaning may have come from someone or some group who lived five hundred years ago. This partisanship leads to creedolatry, a neologism, an excessive veneration for church tradition. Putting church tradition before God's commandments is Phariseeism (Mark 7:9). Paradoxically, Christian "knowledge" is like oxygen. On the one hand, it is essential; on the other hand, too much of it can poison you. Knowledge can become the "noisy gong" and the "clanging symbol" of an intellectualized Christian faith, when what really matters is "faith working through love" (Gal 5:6). Working, not thinking, is the key word.

---

24. Gadamer, *Truth and Method*, 269.

25. "For now we see in a mirror dimly, but then face to face; now I know in part, but then I will know fully just as I also have been fully known."

Finally, the problem of intellectualism is neither hypothetical nor theoretical. The following story shows what I have been describing in this book—a real-world example of the dying and rebirth of an existential Christian life. The story comes from *A Distant Grief*, a book about the martyrdom of Christians in Uganda.

The author, F. Kefa Sempangi, pastored a large church in Uganda that became a target for Idi Amin's campaign of mass murder, terror, and genocide against Christians. In part, the book describes what life is like when you know that someone can murder you at any moment and know that when you go to bed at night, you might not see the dawn. At the same time, the story shows what happens when Christians focus on theological abstractions and the emptiness that follows. The story begins after Sempangi and his family escaped from Uganda and came to America, where he enrolled at Westminster Seminary in Philadelphia.

They are now free from the minute-by-minute fear of death. They enjoy peace for the first time. But what happens to Sempangi's spirit at the seminary? I quote this at length because it describes this book's message about the poverty of intellectualism and the dangers of abstractions.

Here is how Sempangi describes life in Uganda:

> For two years we had lived in constant fear, unable to think of the future. All around us friends had disappeared, prominent citizens had been murdered, whole villages had been massacred. We never knew when our own time would come, and with bodies that shook at the sound of falling leaves, we had no energy to think of the future. Instead, like God's children in the wilderness, we learned to pray only for enough manna to get through the day.[26]

Terror haunted constantly, and they could only cry out to God for help and rely on his promises. But they escaped to Philadelphia, and Sempangi entered seminary.

In his second year at seminary, however, Sempangi noticed that his spiritual life had changed. In Uganda he and his wife read the Bible for hope and life, to hear God's promises and his commands and to obey them. He did not have time for theological arguments. But seminary changed him. As he explains:

> Now, in the security of a new life and with the reality of death fading from mind, I found myself reading Scripture to analyze texts and speculate about meaning. I came to enjoy abstract

26. Sempangi, *Distant Grief*, 178.

theological discussions with my fellow students and, while these discussions were intellectually refreshing, it wasn't long before our fellowship revolved around ideas rather than the work of God in our lives. It was not the blood of Jesus Christ that gave us unity, but our agreement on doctrinal issues. We came together not for confession and forgiveness but for debate.[27]

The downfall of intellectualism comes from prioritizing a system. Knowledge about God replaces knowing God. This is the aesthetic. More doctrine, more system theology did not inspire him to action; it drained his spirit. Sempangi describes its effect: "God Himself had become a distant figure. He had become a subject of debate, an abstract category. I no longer prayed to Him as a living Father but as an impersonal being who did not mind my inattention and unbelief."[28]

But one night Sempangi recognized his sin. He recognized he had turned those closest to him into abstractions when he prayed. And from that night on, his "prayers became specific. I prayed for real people, with real needs. And it was not long before, once again, these needs became the means by which I came face to face with the living God."[29]

Seminary had promoted a system of theological abstractions that turned people and God into abstractions. It produced debaters. The intellectual replaced the existential, the mind became preeminent, and his faith became solipsistic. This is an example of the intellectualism that I have been describing. Systems can petrify the tree of faith and render it fruitless, as Sempangi's life shows. Sempangi became captive to a system, the title of the next chapter.

---

27. Sempangi, *Distant Grief*, 179.
28. Sempangi, *Distant Grief*, 180.
29. Sempangi, *Distant Grief*, 180.

Chapter 12 **Problems with a System —Captive to a System**

WHY DO PASTORS PREACH strong sermons with robust theology yet end up with what they don't want, didn't expect, and can't explain? And why do they keep making the same mistakes? Friedrich Hayek, another conservative commentator on political ideologies, explains that "we are the captives of the ideas we have created."[1] Similarly, churches and denominations can become captive to their theology. Denominations are like nations; they create patriots who see the denomination's strengths but are blind to its weaknesses.

For example, at least some of the problems in this evangelical hypergrace era can be explained by an overemphasis on the doctrine of justification by faith. This overemphasis makes it harder to understand the apostle James's statement that faith without works is dead (Jas 2:17). And unlike John Calvin, many Presbyterians find talking about works quite uncomfortable. But overemphasizing justification by faith can result in shortchanging the importance of regeneration, sanctification, bodily resurrection, and "work[ing] out your salvation with fear and trembling" (Phil 2:12). The key is that Christ died for believers and was resurrected into newness of life. Believers die with Christ and are resurrected into new life. This new life is much more than going to heaven when you die.[2] It is a new life of good works empowered by the Spirit. This overemphasis on justification confuses historical and cultural views for biblical truth.

---

1. Hayek, *Road to Serfdom*, 58.
2. See generally Rom 6.

The result: a concealing follows overemphasizing justification by faith, and problems flow from this concealing, like a phantom view of human responsibility before God.[3] Pastors become reluctant to preach on the human will and works and what it means to persevere in the faith. But too much focus on one biblical doctrine can lead to misunderstanding other biblical truths. Can you say that justification by faith is more important than regeneration? The apostle John wouldn't agree. (See, for example, John 3:3.)

Of course, zealous proponents of doctrine will argue that understanding their system brings action. But if that is true, why are there so many Bourgeois Christians in churches that teach sound doctrine? How do they explain the frozen chosen? Why is it that 10 percent of church members do 90 percent of the church work? Why is it that approximately 25 percent of Americans claim to be Evangelicals, but only about 7–9 percent have a real Christian witness, and most of them are over age sixty?[4] Why do some Evangelicals have so much knowledge and so little love and grace? Why does the term "downtown church" express reproach? Why does Carl Trueman say that "we confessional types are no more immune to the wider cultural waters in which we swim than the mega-church people and the emergents"?[5] Why does Trueman also say that the culture can subvert traditional, confessional Protestantism? Why is there so much privatized religion? Filling up with knowledge can lead to an empty tank of action. This knowledge versus action is part of the Cartesian dualism.

Philosopher Charles Taylor explains that Cartesian dualism leads to seeing reality in a representational way. That means "to know reality is to have a correct representation of things—a correct picture within of outer reality."[6] Doctrine is designed to give a correct picture or framework for understanding the Bible. Doctrine can be very helpful. But when knowledge is the goal, people with knowledge become the leaders and the heroes. As a result, you can end up with one-dimensional thinking and one-dimensional Christians. To the contrary, good behavior and doing good deeds show true wisdom (Jas 3:13).

---

3. The focus on justification by faith follows, in part, the Reformed Tradition. Recent bright lights of Calvinism like Geerhardus Vos, Herman Ridderbos, and Richard Gaffin argue that the true focus of Paul's theology is on the bodily resurrection of Christ and the bodily resurrection of believers that unites them with Christ in an organic unity (Gaffin, *Resurrection and Redemption*, 13).

4. Wells, *Courage to Be Protestant*, 43.

5. Trueman, "Courageous Protestantism?," para. 2.

6. Taylor, *Sources of the Self*, 144.

But doctrine is not what ultimately matters; God's action is. Indeed, as Westminster Seminary Professor Richard B. Gaffin notes: "God's speech is invariably related to his actions."[7] For example, the doctrine of the incarnation is true, but what matters is that the incarnation happened, and only because it happened is the doctrine true. The doctrine didn't happen, because doctrines can't happen. A doctrinal statement about the incarnation is like a label, and you don't buy a bottle of wine for the label. Moreover, doctrinal statements are like blueprints for a house, and although blueprints are helpful, you can't live in a blueprint.

People are not abstractions, our neighbors are not abstractions, and life is not an abstraction. Life is action. The Bourgeois Christian goal of having the correct picture or correct representations of biblical truth in the mind leads to a pagan, Enlightenment view of truth and deep worldliness. How does the Enlightenment view affect believers?

As Charles Taylor explains: "The Enlightenment developed a conception of nature, including human nature, as a set of objectified facts with which the subject had to deal in acquiring knowledge and acting."[8] Also, this Enlightenment concept set up a "kind of abstraction, introducing a false world of representation which cuts man off from the real living sources."[9] Importantly, God did not give his children some denominational doctrine about Christ. First, he gave them Christ, and then he gave them the Gospel of John. Likewise, the church has the doctrine of God, which varies depending on one's denomination. But is a doctrine about God better than the Psalms that describe David's relationship to his God? Theology is like having a picture of your two-year-old grandson. The Christian life is like playing with your grandson.

And as the eighteenth-century Pietist Count Zinzendorf says: "Whoso wishes to grasp God with his intellect becomes an atheist."[10] Zinzendorf, a leader in the German Pietism movement, was tired of theological disputes that characterized much of eighteenth-century Lutheranism and that had sapped the spiritual life out of the Reformation. He emphasized faith, love, and community over dogma. Yet intellectualism remains today as one of the Reformation's unfortunate consequences. But as Kierkegaard says, "Faith, then, is not a lesson for slow learners in the sphere of intellectuality.

---

7. Gaffin, *Resurrection and Redemption*, 22.
8. Taylor, *Hegel*, 22.
9. Taylor, *Hegel*, 24.
10. Taylor, *Secular Age*, 314.

... But faith is a sphere of its own, and the immediate identifying mark of every misunderstanding of Christianity is that it changes it into a doctrine and draws it into the range of intellectuality."[11]

The over-rationalized and systematized truth of Bourgeois Christianity tampers with Christian duty. It extracts a toll on the spiritual traffic of love in God's kingdom. And as sociologist Eva Illouz explains: "Rationalization . . . is the process of expansion of formal systems of knowledge, which in turn lead to an 'intellectualization' of everyday life."[12] The Christian life is everyday life, and theologies are formal systems. The problem, however, is that "the theology you live out is much more important to your daily life than the theology you claim to believe."[13]

Rationalism's main failure in the biblical context is that human reason and human logic are fallen and degraded by sin. Hence, the human mind has serious limits. Finite people cannot understand the infinite and eternal God. Indeed, Dutch Calvinist theologian Herman Bavinck says that we cannot understand the great mystery of who God is. What God has revealed in Scripture about himself far surpasses what we can comprehend.[14] So trying to gain theological certainty about God in a religion based on faith and shrouded in mystery is not a pagan paradox; it is a Christian paradox. And as the Bible explains: "Oh, the depth of the riches both of the wisdom and knowledge of God! How unsearchable are His judgments and unfathomable His ways!" (Rom 11:33). Although these rationalized, representational systems may offer accurate statements of biblical truths, they are not the incarnating and embodying of truth that Jesus requires of his followers. Doctrine has no body. Words can't walk, and in our age, language is too often substituted for being.[15] (Political correctness is a good example of this.)

So contrary to Wells's view about strong preaching, the rains of robust theology can pour down on a congregation of Bourgeois Christians, but it remains a desert without fruit, because for Bourgeois Christians, knowledge is not the way to spirituality; it is spirituality. But as J. Gresham Machen says, "An intellectual conviction of the truth of Christianity is

---

11. Kierkegaard, *Concluding Unscientific Postscript*, 1:327.
12. Illouz, *Cold Intimacies*, 32.
13. Winter, *Heart of the Matter*, 41.
14. Bavinck, *Doctrine of God*, 18.
15. Jaspers, *Man in the Modern Age*, 128. Jaspers says: "Today no attempt is made to use language as a means of contemplating being, language being substituted for being."

always accompanied by a change of heart and a new direction for the will."[16] Machen follows John Calvin here.

Calvin lays the foundation for the Protestant religion. He connects important biblical truths into a clear system, and in many ways, it is the guidebook for Protestantism. But Calvin does something important in the *Institutes* that separates him from contemporary neo-Calvinists. He makes an unequivocal statement about the duty to sacrifice for God's covenant kingdom.[17] As he warns, believers "ought to prepare themselves for a hard, toilsome, and unquiet life, crammed with very many and various kinds of evil."[18] He further explains that God leads his children into eternal life by "the race of good works."[19] Calvin calls for an existential, not an intellectual, Christianity, and his existential call ties into the death and resurrection of Jesus.

William Hendriksen also follows Calvin on the importance of works for the Christian life. He quotes St. Paul's call for increasing in the knowledge of God saying, "So that you will walk in a manner worthy of the Lord, to please Him in all respects, bearing fruit in every good work and increasing in the knowledge of God" (Col 1:10). About these verses William Hendriksen explains: "Now the knowledge here referred to is no abstract, theoretical learning. Such merely theoretical knowledge might be possessed by any nominal Christian,"[20] or as I describe them, by Bourgeois Christians. This knowledge is "heart-transforming and life-renewing."[21] According to Hendriksen, it follows then that "there must be nothing half-hearted about this manner of life."[22] This demands the faith of Heb 12:1—fast feet. And finally, about this passage, Hendriksen explains that "Paul attaches high value to good works viewed as the fruit—not the root—of grace."[23]

In conclusion, nothing that I say in this book should imply that I'm against theological systems or sound doctrine. Both are important and

16. Machen, *What Is Faith?*, 135.

17. See, for example, Calvin, *Institutes*, 1:698: "Rather, each man will so consider with himself that in all his greatness he is a debtor to his neighbors, and that he ought in exercising kindness toward them to set no other limit than the end of his resources; these, as widely as they are extended, ought to have their limits set according to the rule of love."

18. Calvin, *Institutes*, 1:702.

19. Calvin, *Institutes*, 1:821.

20. Hendriksen, *Commentary on Colossians*, 56.

21. Hendriksen, *Commentary on Colossians*, 57.

22. Hendriksen, *Commentary on Colossians*, 57.

23. Hendriksen, *Commentary on Colossians*, 58.

helpful. I'm opposed to them when they are misused or overemphasized. Nothing that I say disputes the reality that the Christian life is based on God's grace, mercy, and love. But as I note in the introduction, Plato and Western rationalism are still behind the scenes pulling strings, and by that I mean that Evangelicals cannot see how pagan philosophy still drags down the church. Sad indeed go those who sort out all the theology and doctrine only to miss what it means to be a Christian.

Chapter 13 Christian Ethics: From the Beginning to the End

"Duty" is a word that many Evangelicals don't like. They don't like it because they believe their duty to God mostly stops when they accept Christ as their Savior. Or they think that the idea of duty disparages grace. But Christian ethics and the duties that arise therefrom are primordial, from the beginning and of the first order, and that ethical order continues through the ages and commands believers to the end at judgment day.

Once again for this chapter, I have chosen a word, "ethics," to avoid the clichés common in evangelical churches. For many Evangelicals' ears, it is awkward to hear about ethics and duty when they have been trained to hear only grace. Grace is comfortable; duty is tough. But as Oxford philosopher and novelist Iris Murdoch explains: "The idea of a network of ordinary duties is an extremely important aspect of morals, it goes with a sense of being always on duty, a conscript not a gentlemen volunteer."[1]

A network of duties structures the Christian life, and duties are very important for believers. Duties flow from the law of God. Likewise, being conscripted into an army describes Christians who are called to fight the good fight of faith while wearing the full armor of God (Eph 6:13; 1 Tim 6:12).

The word *primordial* describes what happened in the beginning, and the word *ethics* describes the system or ethical order that God established in the beginning. This primordial pattern recurs in Scripture as part of the unfolding history of redemption. Importantly, ethics is part of God's redemptive plan, but it is not the basis for that plan. The basis rests in God's

---

1. Murdoch, *Metaphysics as a Guide*, 383.

love, mercy, and grace and in Jesus's sacrificial death, resurrection, and redemption. The plan begins in Genesis.

The Genesis account shows that God's ethical system began with the creation ordinances. God created Adam and put him in the garden to tend it, and Adam used his body to do the work. God also commanded Adam not to eat from the tree of the knowledge of good and evil. He created Adam, put him to work, and gave him commands about what he should and should not do (Gen 2:7–9, 15–17).

This is a prototype for ethical systems. A prototype includes an authority establishing an order for living (God), those who receive the authority's order (humanity), rules for human conduct, and the call to obey. The simplicity of the Genesis account develops throughout the Bible into the density of the full-orbed calling of believers in Christ. Duty necessarily entails the will to work. But something else is primordial and easy to miss.

God gave Adam life and a place to live in the garden. After giving him these gifts, God gave commands. God's action in the beginning parallels and foreshadows God's gracious action in giving believers new life and a new abode in another garden called the kingdom of God. The commands about how to live the new life in the new abode follow the gift giving. In fact, the commands are also gifts because they show the way to blessing. The commands call on the heart, mind, and body to respond.

The body centers the Christian life just as Christ's body satisfied the atonement. And as Merleau-Ponty describes it: "My body is the fabric into which all objects are woven, and it is, at least in relation to the perceived world, the general instrument of my 'comprehension'. It is my body which gives significance not only to the natural object, but also to cultural objects like words."[2] Believers' bodies animate biblical truth just as Jesus's incarnate body did. Believers use their bodies to love neighbors. To state the obvious: without a body, a preacher can't preach. And there is more.

How can you understand God's love without parents? How can you understand the doctrine of adoption without parents who adopt children (Gal 4:5)? How can you understand that the church is the bride of Christ without people getting married (Rev 19:7)? How can you understand the Eucharist in which Christ's body, symbolized by the bread, is broken for believers (Matt 26:26)? All this happens with bodies in action.

Unfortunately, Bourgeois Christians rarely think that the body is essential for serving God, which again demonstrates the power of

---

2. Merleau-Ponty, *Phenomenology of Perception*, 273.

the Cartesian world-picture that holds them captive and their belief in the primacy of the intellect for serving God. They don't recognize that a believer's new creation in Christ described in Eph 2:10 is an "ethical renewal."[3] Life before renewal in Christ is a life of walking in sins. New life in Christ is a life of walking in good works.[4] The body walks in good works. The believer's body is resurrected with Christ's body, and an organic unity results. And as Professor Gaffin explains: "Resurrection with Christ likewise involves an existential component. The believer's continuing walk in newness of life is based upon resurrection with Christ as that has taken place in his actual life history."[5]

But Charles Taylor describes the problem well: "Official Christianity has gone through what we call an 'excarnation', a transfer out of embodied, 'enfleshed' forms of religious life, to those which are more 'in the head'. In this it follows in parallel with 'Enlightenment', and modern unbelieving culture in general."[6] For example, some years ago while sight-seeing in Paris at L'Église St. Germain des Pres, I read a sign on the church wall that said in French, "Christianity is a religion of the body." It immediately struck me that I would never see this sign in a Protestant church in America. The sign spoke truth but not the truth normally found in evangelical churches. But the Christian life is like football; it is a contact sport. You need armor for it. Indeed, one sociologist of American Evangelicalism describes evangelical action as more symbolic than practical in shaping their actions.[7]

Furthermore, ethics are not just primordial; ethics are apocalyptical. Their force and duties last until the end, and the end is when time stops and judgment comes. We think of time as something astronomical based on the Earth moving around the Sun. But time is a place that God gives Christians to love neighbors and to do the good works that he prepared beforehand for them to do. Time is spatial.

---

3. Gaffin, *Resurrection and Redemption*, 43.

4. Gaffin, *Resurrection and Redemption*, 43. Gaffin describes this as an "about-face."

5. Gaffin, *Resurrection and Redemption*, 47. Gaffin further says: "There is no element in the whole of Paul's soteriology more basic than this existential union with Christ. To treat it in abstraction from or to the exclusion of the ideas that believers have been chosen eternally in Christ and were contemplated as one with Christ at the time of his sufferings, death and resurrection would of course radically distort Paul's perspective. The predestinarian, the past historical and the existential 'in Christ' are indissolubly connected" (51).

6. Taylor, *Secular Age*, 554.

7. Wuthnow, *Crisis in the Churches*, 227.

Furthermore, Christianity is teleological because God has a goal, a plan, and an end—his plan of redemption, not just for people, but for the whole creation. And most importantly, he is the End (Rev 1:8; 21:6). He is the End as the guide and the End as the goal. But his children play an essential role in the plan, and he guides them to this End. Teleology implies the power to execute the plan and see it through, and he empowers his children to implement the plan through vital union with Christ. God's teleology includes believers' responsibility to follow God's law. And as Anglican theologian John R. W. Stott explains in *Christian Counter-Culture*: "So we have no liberty to try to dodge or duck the lofty demands of the law. Law-dodging is a pharisaic hobby; what is characteristic of Christians is a keen appetite for righteousness, hungering and thirsting after it continuously."[8] God has jobs for his children to do in the space called time.

God's redemptive plan in Christ is also eschatological. Eschatology focuses on the bodily resurrection of Christ that leads to and makes possible the bodily resurrection of all believers who will get new bodies. Professor Gaffin explains the significance of the resurrection: "Christ's resurrection . . . is the beginning of the 'general epochal event' which at the same time makes him head over the others; with his resurrection is given the resurrection of believers."[9] He further says that this takes place for believers existentially.[10] As part of the new birth, the dying and rising from the dead with Christ, new believers should yield their lives to God and their bodies as instruments of righteousness to God (Rom 6:13). This is regeneration and the power that comes with it.[11]

So what happens at the end? Paul describes it in Rom 2:6–8. It is the judgment of God, "who will render to each person according to his deeds: to those who by perseverance in doing good seek for glory and honor and immortality, eternal life; but to those who are selfishly ambitious and do not

---

8. Stott, *Christian Counter-Culture*, 124.

9. Gaffin, *Resurrection and Redemption*, 38.

10. Gaffin, *Resurrection and Redemption*, 42.

11. Simpson and Bruce, *Commentary on the Epistles*, 56. These theologians offer a striking description of the people who deny the power of regeneration. "There are good works likewise made ready for our performance. Lie-a-bed slackers, alas! Eager to be cosily fondled, but loth to do a day's work in the Master's vineyard, half-breeds at best, are only too common. Many Christians contrive to spend their lives in canvassing the question, 'Lord, what wilt thou have me to do?' and having made extensive preparations for living to good purpose, end their days 'caught napping,' a prey to chronic indecision, inmates of the Castle of Indolence to the last."

obey the truth, but obey unrighteousness, wrath and indignation." There is tribulation for those who do evil and "glory and honor and peace" for those who do good (Rom 2:9–10). At the judgment of the great white throne, people are judged according to their deeds, not how emotional they were when they accepted Christ as their Savior.[12] Ethics and deeds go together, and deeds are done in a body as Christ's deeds were done in his incarnate body. Deeds don't save; deeds show those who are saved.

But as contemporary French philosopher Pierre Manent explains, obligations that people must fulfill with their bodies create problems in a democracy, because democracy is about individual freedom—freedom from bonds and obligations like loving your neighbor or loving your wife. Neighbor duty limits freedom. (Remember that in this book "democracy" is a social system and not a form of government.)

According to Manent, because democracy is about individual liberty, and because undertaking duties and obligations strikes against personal liberty, such duties can only arise from the individual's consent.[13] It follows that a person can withdraw that consent to an obligation at any time to return to freedom from the duty. It is easy to see how this works out in the culture. Our democracy dissolves marital obligations by consent-ending, no-fault divorce. Likewise, bodily duty is limited in sexual relations in the hookup culture that requires only a few hot moments of pleasure. Abortion frees sexual pleasure from the duty to children. Being a father requires a bodily relationship with your children. Fertilizing a woman's egg and abandoning your offspring requires no bond other than brief clutching and rolling in a bed. This culture has released people to erotic pleasures without obliging them to family duties. The body is free for self-indulgence.

Moreover, technology, especially social media, enables bodiless relations with others on the internet. No responsibilities or duties arise from the social media "relationship." You can lie, deceive, or bully on social media without suffering consequences. Hence, in denying the body's importance in ministry, Bourgeois Christians follow the pipers of the age when they limit the role of the body in the Christian life.

Manent further explains, "I can show you that in reality in the history of the West, our society is the one that most systematically reduces the

---

12. Years ago, I had lunch with a well-known apologist/evangelist, and I asked him how many people who made professions of faith at his meetings did he believe were actually saved. He said 10 percent.

13. Manent, *Cours familier de philosophie politique*, 191–92. (These are my translations.)

importance and role of the body, the one that disregards it the most."[14] It has not always been this way. The Book of Common Prayer was originally written in the sixteenth century. As part of the marriage vows and the exchange of rings, the couple says: "With this ring I marry you, with *my body* I honor you, and with all my worldly goods I share: In the name of the Father, and of the Son, and of the Holy Spirit. Amen."[15] Centuries ago people understood the importance of the body for marriage. The vow shows this understanding and consents to the duty. I can explain the consent and loss of freedom with a simple example. For ten years before I married my wife, I dated different women whom I found attractive. But in my wedding vows, I committed to her and gave up my freedom to date. It was a spiritual commitment and a bodily commitment.

Finally, in further describing the character of the age, Manent offers a striking metaphor. "We conduct ourselves, or rather, because life is more complicated, we would like to conduct ourselves like angels, who by some chance have a body, and who are free to cast it off and take it up at will."[16] When I first translated this, I thought Manent meant that people want to be good like angels. But that is not it. People in the democratic age want to be like angels because angels have no bodies. People want to be free of bodily duties and bonds that restrict their freedom. If they obligate themselves, they want to be able to terminate those obligations at will. When Bourgeois Christians deny the importance of loving their neighbors, they show themselves caught up in the emptiness of the age in a bodiless but intellectualized Christianity.

But ethics require actions within a community, and the most concise example of that is the Ten Commandments. God gave Moses the Ten Commandments for God's people to follow, but most Evangelicals only half understand their importance. They recognize that they should not sin, and that means avoiding what God prohibits. But they fail to understand that the Ten Commandments are not just for their relationship with God; they also protect the community. They stabilize the community by describing how to treat others and forbid acts and thoughts that destroy community and people's lives. After all, you can't murder God, lie to him,

---

14. Manent, *Cours familier de philosophie politique*, 223.

15. Anglican Church in North America, *Book of Common Prayer*, 212. Emphasis added. I thank Professor Carl Trueman for this reference.

16. Manent, *Cours familier de philosophie politique*, 231.

steal from him, or sleep with his wife, but you can harm people in those ways, and such harm disrupts community.

Killing, lying, stealing, and sleeping with another man's wife disrupt relationships. Envy and covetousness stir up these sins. Indeed, worshipping other gods, the commandment that seems to apply only to God, also disrupts community. We see that in the Middle East with the Jews and the Palestinians and the Sunnis and the Shiites. God's commandments are not just between God and the individual. They establish a system of duties that organize and integrate the covenant community and the broader human community in peace. And finally, a community is always a group of bodies living together, not a collection of minds.

I end this chapter with this thought. In his essay called "The Word of Nietzsche," Martin Heidegger says that "it could be that Christendom itself represents one consequence and bodying-forth of nihilism."[17] Ravi Zacharias's sin is an example of this bodying forth of nihilism. To the degree that many Evangelicals deny God's regenerative power in their lives and their duty to love their neighbor, they contribute to the nihilism of our secular age, no matter how robust the doctrine is in their churches. In an existential way, they are denying the power of God in an age that believes God has no power. That contributes to nihilism.[18]

Christians overcome nihilism by putting their bodies to work in the kingdom of God. Indeed, the body is "for the Lord, and the Lord is for the body" (1 Cor 6:13). And the body is also for the neighbors God calls you to love. The incarnate, embodied faith of people embedded in a community is the true will to power, through the Holy Spirit, that defeats the nihilism and emptiness of the age. The next chapter, my conclusion, offers some real-world examples.

---

17. Heidegger, *Question Concerning Technology*, 65.

18. In one of my classes, a student asked why millennials have little interest in religion. My best philosophy student, a Christian, said millennials don't go to church because they have looked at the older generation of Evangelicals like their parents and have seen that whatever their profession might be, their religion makes little difference in their lives, so why bother with it. This is the bodying forth of nihilism.

Chapter 14 Conclusion: The Quotidian Christians

THE DAILY CHRISTIANS—WHAT ARE they like and what do they do? They live differently from the once-a-week Christians. They grip the dailiness of life and seize its hourly unfolding by serving others. They live the Rom 12:1 embodied Christian life.

John and Connie, an older couple, serve in an inner-city church in a violent, drug-infested pocket of poverty where black-on-black murder is a common tragedy, where poverty beleaguers, and where fear afflicts the neighborhood. There you find boarded-up crack houses, smoldering violence, and evil lurking in dark places with roaming gangs and street-corner crack sales. John has helped homeless young men find lodging in boarding houses, paid the rent, and helped them buy furniture. He takes them to the grocery store for food and to Wal-Mart for clothes. He helps high school dropouts get GEDs and find jobs. He visits the sick in hospitals, the addicted in rehab centers, and the indicted in jails. He carries disabled women to doctor appointments and then to pharmacies to fill their prescriptions. He shares their grief at funerals, counsels their despair, and encourages the hopeless with the gospel of peace in a neighborhood where there is no peace. For ten years he has taught a weekly Bible study for neighborhood men. Of all the people he has helped, not one of them can repay him except with a thanks, and he often doesn't get that.

For ten years John's wife Connie has taught a weekly women's Bible study for neighborhood women. She has set up monthly luncheons for them. She tutors young girls and counsels mothers who struggle with drug and alcohol abuse. She drives students to school and brings them home.

She takes sick women to doctor appointments and emergency rooms and others to grocery stores. She tries to restore broken relationships in families and among neighbors. She invites girls and their mothers into her home to eat and spend the night. For many of them, it is their first time in a white person's home except to work. She goes to ball games to encourage players. She visits the sick in hospitals and the down-trodden in jails.

Jeanne works in the same inner-city church. She started the Heavenly Bakers with several elementary schoolgirls and taught them how to bake, and they sold their cookies at church. She started a Strong Girls program and taught young girls the Bible. She invited them for meals in her home, and the girls helped cook and then spent the night. Over the years they have watched movies together and taken field trips. Jeanne read an inner-city version of *Pilgrim's Progress* and other Christian books to the girls. She has mentored them, counseled them about school and family problems, and warned about drug abuse and unwanted pregnancies. All the girls live in pinching poverty with single moms.

Another member of this inner-city church has cooked meals for church members, carried water to them on hot summer days, served food at church dinners, and preached occasionally to give the pastor a break. He sometimes drives the church van for members who have no ride to church. He has visited them in jails and half-way houses.

Doyle, in his mid-forties with a young family, runs a tree service. He and other young men went to the town's largest public housing project and started a soccer ministry without knowing anyone there or anything about soccer. Doyle saw this as a way to reach the children with the gospel. He came to know and work with Ty, a young elementary school boy living with a single mom and many brothers and sisters. Ty became an excellent soccer player, and Doyle brought him into his home as one of his children and sends him to a private school where he stars in soccer.

Ellen, a member of a large Presbyterian church and the mother of five children and grandmother of ten, has taken meals to new mothers in the church for twenty years. She also takes the newborn a Bible with the child's name embossed on it. She is an excellent baker and takes sourdough bread and cinnamon rolls to the hurting and to encourage people struggling with life's problems. She makes desserts for the Christmas lunch for the widows in the church. She also buys groceries monthly for an elderly shut-in.

Chuck spent years traveling up I-75 to earn a master's degree from Reformed Theological Seminary in Atlanta. After earning the degree, he sold his profitable business and went to work at his church without pay. Every year he goes to Mexico to work in an orphanage built out of an abandoned motel where he loves the kids, and they love him. Over the years he has dug ditches, poured foundations, sledge-hammered rock, and laid concrete block to build dormitories and a kitchen for the children.

Robin and her husband, Lindsey, have led a Sunday School class for single adults for years. Every week they open their home for Bible study, prayer, and fellowship. They counsel these young adults about job problems and questions about sex, dating, and marriage. They answer tough questions about life and being a Christian. Foremost, they encourage young people who are starting to make their way in life.

DeAnn is an older woman, a widow, in a Midwestern town. She leads a Bible study at a Jewish retirement center every week. She mentors a young woman recently out of prison and volunteers weekly at a youth ranch for children in foster care. She adds all this to her church ministry.

Carrie, a young mother with two children who lives in New York City, goes to a dangerous Bronx neighborhood several times a week to help run parenting classes at a ministry called A House on Beekman. Half of the time, she cares for the children who come with their mothers. The rest of the time she teaches the moms how to nurture their children.

Sah, a Harvard-educated architect in Manhattan, works with Habitat for Humanity building houses. Emily is a physician's assistant who leads a Bible study for medical students. Glenn is a businessman who manages a ministry called Overcoming Job Transition that offers support and training to people who have lost their jobs. Gary, a busy landscaper with three children, started a prison ministry in the local jail and takes the gospel to prisoners. He has hired some of them to work for him.

All these people are working in the kingdom of God for the King. All these believers are using their skills, gifts, and experience to help others as a regular part of life because of their love for God and their desire to obey him by serving others. This requires time, energy, money, and bodily presence. They are walking the narrow way to "an eternal weight of glory far beyond all comparison" (2 Cor 4:17). The narrow way is the blessed way.

Jesus calls his disciples to walk the narrow way (Matt 7:13). There was a narrow way on the road between Jericho and Jerusalem where a robbed and beaten man lay dying. A priest and a Levite took the broad way on this road and walked around him. The Samaritan took the narrow way, stopped, and helped him. The narrow way on this road has nothing to do with the width of the road. It describes the duty of Christian love owed to a dying and helpless man. Many broad ways lead to destruction, and people travel them to avoid serving: the way of indifference, the way of callousness, the way of pride, the way of sloth, the way of fear, the way of complacency, the way of inconvenience, and the procrastinating way. Broad ways are false ways that arise from being preoccupied with oneself.

The evangelical church needs more narrow-way, wound-binding Samaritans. Our neighbors' wounds are physical, mental, and emotional, like loneliness, despair, and anxiety. Evangelicals must learn that God wants more from his children than learning the Bible and avoiding sin. He calls them to help their neighbors, which means loving them sacrificially as Christ loved the church. God calls them to live a grace-charged, love-glowing life. Christ is not just Savior and Lord; he exemplified the Rom 12:1 life that Christians should live.

Finally, Evangelicals should learn from the COVID-19 epidemic that people need other people, and that need is an essential part of being human. We all need love. And we should pray to God as the psalmist did: "Let me hear Your lovingkindness in the morning; For I trust in You; Teach me the way in which I should walk" (Ps 143:8). And during the day, walk in Jesus's way to love our neighbors because as he says, "Whoever believes in me will do the works I do" (John 14:12 ESV). To that end, call on God as St. Augustine did: "Up, Lord, and do; stir us up, and recall us; kindle and draw us; inflame, grow sweet unto us; let us now love, let us run."[1] And while we run, remember that "we love because he first loved us" (1 John 4:19).

---

1. Augustine, *Confessions*, 151.

Bibliography

Adorno, Theodor. *Minima Moralia: Reflections on a Damaged Life*. Translated by E. F. N. Jephcott. New York: Verso, 2005.
Arendt, Hannah. *Between Past and Future: Eight Exercises in Political Thought*. Penguin Classics. New York: Penguin, 2006.
———. *The Human Condition*. Chicago: University of Chicago Press, 1998.
Aristotle. *Metaphysics, Books 1–9*. Edited by G. P. Gould. Translated by Hugh Tredennick. LCL. Cambridge, MA: Harvard University Press, 1980.
———. *Nicomachean Ethics*. Translated by Robert C. Bartlett and Susan D. Collins. Chicago: University of Chicago Press, 2012.
Augustine. *The City of God*. Translated by Marcus Dods. New York: Random House, 1950.
———. *The Confessions of Saint Augustine*. Translated by Edward B. Pusey. New York: Random House, 1949.
Baugh, Stephen M. "Kittel and Biblical Theology: A Review." Kerux, Sept. 1988. http://kerux.com/doc/0302R1.asp.
Bavinck, Herman. *The Doctrine of God*. Edited and translated by William Hendriksen. Carlisle, PA: Banner of Truth, 1977.
Bellah, Robert N., et al. *Habits of the Heart: Individualism and Commitment in American Life*. New York: Perennial Library, Harper & Row, 1986.
Berlin, Isaiah. *The Roots of Romanticism*. Edited by Henry Hardy. Princeton, NJ: Princeton University Press, 2013.
Anglican Church in North America. *The Book of Common Prayer and Administration of the Sacraments with Other Rites and Ceremonies of the Church*. Huntington Beach, CA: Anglican Liturgy, 2019.
Brown, John. *Hebrews*. Carlisle, PA: Banner of Truth, 1976.
Buber, Martin. *I and Thou*. Translated by Walter Kaufmann. New York: Simon & Schuster, 1970.
Calvin, John. *Institutes of the Christian Religion*. Edited by John T. McNeill. Translated by Ford Lewis Battles. 2 vols. Philadelphia: Westminster, 1960.
Candlish, Robert S. *A Commentary on 1 John*. Avon, Eng.: Bath, 1993.
Coleridge, Samuel Taylor. *Poems and Prose*. New York: Knopf, 1997.

Committee for Christian Education & Publications. *The Westminster Confession of Faith Together with the Larger Catechism and the Shorter Catechism with the Scripture Proofs.* Atlanta: Committee for Christian Education & Publications, 1990.

Constant, Benjamin. *The Liberty of Ancients Compared with That of Moderns.* Liberty Fund, 1819. https://oll.libertyfund.org/titles/2251.

Cragg, G. R. *From Puritanism to the Age of Reason: A Study of Changes in Religious Thought Within the Church of England, 1660 to 1700.* Cambridge: Cambridge University Press, 1950.

Descartes, Rene. *"Discourse on Method" and "Meditations on First Philosophy."* Translated by Donald A. Cress. 3rd ed. Indianapolis: Hackett, 1980.

———. *Meditations on First Philosophy.* Edited and translated by John Cottingham. Cambridge Texts in the History of Philosophy. Cambridge: Cambridge University Press, 1999.

Dieleman, Karen. *Religious Imaginaries: The Liturgical and Poetic Practices of Elizabeth Barrett Browning, Christina Rossetti, and Adelaide Proctor.* Athens, OH: Ohio University Press, 2012.

Dreyfus, Hubert, and Charles Taylor. *Retrieving Realism.* Cambridge, MA: Harvard University Press, 2015.

Dumont, Louis. *Essays on Individualism: Modern Ideology in Anthropological Perspective.* Chicago: University of Chicago Press, 1992.

Dupré, Louis. "The Sickness unto Death: Critique of the Modern Age." In *Sickness unto Death,* edited by Robert L. Perkins, 85–119. Vol. 19 of *International Kierkegaard Commentary.* Macon: Mercer University Press, 2007.

Farnsworth, Hal. "Is It Too Much to Ask?" Presentation at "Our Mission and Our Challenging World" conference, First Presbyterian Church, Macon, Feb. 18, 2024.

Ferry, Luc. *Homo Aestheticus: The Invention of Taste in the Democratic Age.* Translated by Robert de Loaiza. Chicago: University of Chicago Press, 1993.

Frame, John M. "Machen's Warrior Children." Works of John Frame & Vern Poythress, June 6, 2012. From *Alister E. McGrath and Evangelical Theology,* edited by Sung Wook Chung (Grand Rapids: Baker, 2003). http://www.frame-poythress.org/machens-warrior-children/.

Furedi, Frank. *Therapy Culture: Cultivating Vulnerability in an Uncertain Age.* New York: Routledge, 2004.

Gadamer, Hans-Georg. *Truth and Method.* Edited by John Cumming and Garrett Barden. Translated by W. Glen-Doepel. New York: Continuum, 2006.

Gaffin, Richard B., Jr. *Resurrection and Redemption: A Study in Paul's Soteriology.* Phillipsburg, NJ: Presbyterian and Reformed, 1987.

Gardner, Stephen L. "The Eros and Ambitions of Psychological Man." In *The Triumph of the Therapeutic: Uses of Faith After Freud,* 225–45. Wilmington, DE: ISI, 2007.

Gauchet, Marcel. *The Disenchantment of the World: A Political History of Religion.* Translated by Oscar Burge. Princeton, NJ: Princeton University Press, 1999.

Gillespie, Michael Allen. *Nihilism Before Nietzsche.* Chicago: University of Chicago Press, 1996.

Goethe, Johann Wolfgang von. *Italian Journey [1786–88].* Translated by W. H. Auden and Elizabeth Mayer. Penguin Classics. New York: Penguin Classics, 1970.

Goldwin, Robert A. "John Locke." In *History of Political Philosophy,* edited by Leo Strauss and Joseph Cropsey, 451–86. Chicago: Rand McNally, 1972.

Guinness, Os. *Fit Bodies Fat Minds: Why Evangelicals Don't Think and What to Do About It*. Grand Rapids: Hourglass, 1994.
———. *The Gravedigger File*. London: Hodder and Stoughton, 1983.
Hart, David Bentley. *Atheist Delusions: The Christian Revolution and Its Fashionable Enemies*. New Haven, CT: Yale University Press, 2009.
Hayek, F. A. *The Road to Serfdom*. Edited by Bruce Caldwell. Vol. 2 of *The Collected Works of F. A. Hayek*. Chicago: University of Chicago Press, 2007.
Hegel, G. W. F. *Elements of the Philosophy of Right*. Edited by Allen W. Wood. Translated by H. B. Nisbet. New York: Cambridge University Press, 2010.
———. *Phenomenology of Spirit*. Translated by A. V. Miller. New York: Oxford University Press, 1977.
Heidegger, Martin. *The Fundamental Concepts of Metaphysics: World, Finitude, Solitude*. Translated by William McNeill and Nicholas Walker. Bloomington: Indiana University Press, 1995.
———. "The Fundamental Question of Metaphysics." In *Philosophy in the Twentieth Century: An Anthology*, edited by William Barrett and Henry D. Aiken, 3:219–50. New York: Random House, 1962.
———. *Holderlin's Hymn "The Ister."* Translated by William McNeill and Julia Davis. Bloomington: Indiana University Press, 1996.
———. *Parmenides*. Translated by Andre Schuwer and Richard Rojcewicz. Bloomington: Indiana University Press, 1998.
———. "Plato's Doctrine of Truth." In *Pathmarks*, translated by William McNeil, 155–82. New York: Cambridge University Press, 1998.
———. *"The Question Concerning Technology" and Other Essays*. Translated by William Lovitt. New York: Harper & Row, 1977.
Helm, Paul. "The Christian Man's Calling." *Banner of Truth* 54 (1968) 21–24.
———. "On Being a Contemporary Christian." *Banner of Truth* 57 (1968) 15–18.
Hendriksen, William. *Commentary on the Epistle to the Colossians*. New Testament Commentary. Grand Rapids: Baker, 1981.
———. *Exposition of the Gospel According to John*. New Testament Commentary. Grand Rapids: Baker, 1979.
———. *Exposition of the Gospel According to Matthew*. New Testament Commentary. Grand Rapids: Baker, 1977.
Hodge, Charles. *A Commentary on 1 & 2 Corinthians*. Carlisle, PA: Banner of Truth, 1978.
———. *Systematic Theology*. 3 vols. Grand Rapids: Eerdmans, 1977.
Horkheimer, Max. *Critique of Instrumental Reason*. Translated by Matthew J. O'Connell et al. Brooklyn, NY: Verso, 2012.
Huxley, Aldous. *Ends and Means: An Enquiry into the Nature of Ideals and into the Methods Employed for Their Realisation*. London: Chatto & Windus, 1946.
Ihde, Don. *Bodies in Technology*. Minneapolis: University of Minnesota Press, 2002.
Illouz, Eva. *Cold Intimacies: The Making of Emotional Capitalism*. Malden, MA: Polity, 2007.
Jacobi, Friedrich Heinrich. *The Main Philosophical Writings and the Novel "Allwill."* Edited and translated by George di Giovanni. McGill-Queen's Studies in the History of Ideas Series 18. Montreal: McGill-Queen's University Press, 2009.
Jacobs, Alan. *A Visit to Vanity Fair: Moral Essays on the Present Age*. Grand Rapids: Brazos, 2001.

Jaspers, Karl. *Karl Jaspers: Basic Philosophical Writings*. Edited and translated by Edith Ehrlich et al. Humanities. Amherst, NY: Humanity, 2000.

———. *Man in the Modern Age*. Translated by Eden Paul and Cedar Paul. London: Routledge, 1951.

———. *Way to Wisdom: An Introduction to Philosophy*. Translated by Ralph Manheim. New Haven, CT: Yale University Press, 2003.

Kierkegaard, Søren. *The Concept of Anxiety: A Simple Psychologically Orienting Deliberation on the Dogmatic Issue of Hereditary Sin*. Edited and translated by Reidar Thomte with Albert B. Anderson. Princeton, NJ: Princeton University Press, 1980.

———. *Concluding Unscientific Postscript to "Philosophical Fragments."* Edited and translated by Howard V. Hong and Edna H. Hong. 2 vols. Kierkegaard's Writings. Princeton, NJ: Princeton University Press, 1992.

———. *Fear and Trembling*. Edited by C. Stephen Evans and Sylvia Walsh. Translated by Sylvia Walsh. New York: Cambridge University Press, 2006.

———. *Kierkegaard's Concluding Unscientific Postscript*. Translated by David F. Swenson and Walter Lowrie. Princeton, NJ: Princeton University Press, 1974.

———. *The Point of View*. Edited and translated by Howard V. Hong and Edna H. Hong. Kierkegaard's Writings. Princeton, NJ: Princeton University Press, 1998.

———. *Two Ages: The Age of Revolution and the Present Age*. Edited and translated by Howard V. Hong and Edna H. Hong. Kierkegaard's Writings. Princeton, NJ: Princeton University Press, 2009.

———. *Upbuilding Discourses in Various Spirits*. Edited and translated by Howard V. Hong and Edna H. Hong. Kierkegaard's Writings. Princeton, NJ: Princeton University Press, 2009.

———. *Works of Love*. Edited and translated by Howard Hong and Edna Hong. New York: Harper Perennial Modern Thought, 2009.

Levinas, Emmanuel. *Alterity and Transcendence*. Translated by Michael B. Smith. New York: Columbia University Press, 1999.

———. *Totality and Infinity: An Essay on Exteriority*. Translated by Alphonso Lingis. Pittsburgh: Duquesne University Press, 2015.

Lloyd-Jones, Martyn. *A First Book of Daily Readings from the Works of Martyn Lloyd-Jones*. Edited by Frank Cumbers. Grand Rapids: Eerdmans, 1983.

Luther, Martin. *Commentary on Romans*. Translated by J. Theodore Mueller. Grand Rapids: Kregel, 1976.

———. *Table Talk*. Translated by William Hazlitt. Gainesville, FL: Bridge-Logos, 2004.

Machen, J. Gresham. *What Is Faith?* Grand Rapids: Eerdmans, 1974.

MacIntyre, Alasdair. *After Virtue: A Study in Moral Theory*. Notre Dame, IN: University of Notre Dame Press, 2007.

Macpherson, C. B. *The Political Theory of Possessive Individualism: Hobbes to Locke*. N.p., Can.: Oxford University Press, 2011.

Manent, Pierre. *Cours familier de philosophie politique*. Mesnil-sur-L'Estrée, Fr.: Gaillmard, 2006.

Merleau-Ponty, Maurice. *Phenomenology of Perception*. Translated by Colin Smith. New York: Routledge, 2009.

More, Robert, Jr. "The Historical Origins of 'the Altar Call.'" *Banner of Truth* 76 (1970) 30–33.

Moskowitz, Eva S. *In Therapy We Trust: America's Obsession with Self-Fulfillment*. Baltimore: Johns Hopkins University Press, 2001.

Murdoch, Iris. *Metaphysics as a Guide to Morals*. New York: Penguin, 1992.
Murray, John J. "We Pray—but Do We?" *Banner of Truth* 65 (1969) 1–3.
Nietzsche, Friedrich. *Beyond Good and Evil: Prelude to a Philosophy of the Future*. Translated by Marion Faber. Oxford World's Classics. New York: Oxford University Press, 2008.
———. *The Gay Science*. Translated by Walter Kaufmann. New York: Vintage, 1974.
———. *On the Genealogy of Morality*. Edited by Keith Ansell-Pearson. Translated by Carole Diethe. 2nd ed. Cambridge Texts in the History of Political Thought. Cambridge: Cambridge University Press, 2007.
———. *Untimely Meditations*. Edited by Daniel Breazeale. Translated by R. J. Hollingdale. Cambridge Texts in the History of Philosophy. New York: Cambridge University Press, 2007.
Noll, Mark A. *The Scandal of the Evangelical Mind*. Grand Rapids: Eerdmans, 1994.
Oakeshott, Michael. *"Rationalism in Politics" and Other Essays*. Rev. ed. Indianapolis: Liberty, 1991.
Ortega y Gasset, José. *"History as a System" and Other Essays Toward a Philosophy of History*. Translated by Helene Weyl. New York: Norton, 1961.
———. *Man and Crisis*. Translated by Mildred Adams. New York: Norton, 1958.
Packer, J. I. *Knowing God*. Downers Grove, IL: InterVarsity, 1993.
Pascal, Blaise. *"Pensées" and Other Writings*. Edited by Anthony Levi. Translated by Honor Levi. Oxford World's Classics. New York: Oxford University Press, 2008.
Piper, John. "Don't Serve God." Desiring God, May 7, 2021. https://www.desiringgod.org/articles/dont-serve-god.
Plato. *Euthyphro. Apology. Crito. Phaedo. Phaedrus*. Edited by G. P. Gould. Translated by Harold North Fowler. Vol. 1 of *Plato in Twelve Volumes*. LCL. Cambridge, MA: Harvard University Press, 1982.
———. *Plato's "Republic."* Translated by G. M. A. Grube. Hackett Classics. Indianapolis: Hackett, 1987.
Plotinus. *Porphyry on Plotinus. Ennead I*. Translated by A. H. Armstrong. LCL. Cambridge, MA: Harvard University Press, 1995.
Plumer, William S. *Psalms: A Critical and Expository Commentary with Doctrinal and Practical Remarks*. Carlisle, PA: Banner of Truth, 1978.
Rehnman, Sebastian. "Alleged Rationalism: Francis Turretin on Reason." *Calvin Theological Journal* 37 (2002) 255–69.
Ridderbos, Herman. *The Coming of the Kingdom*. Edited by Raymond O. Zorn. Translated by H. de Jongste. Philadelphia: Presbyterian and Reformed, 1962.
Rieff, Philip. *The Triumph of the Therapeutic: Uses of Faith After Freud*. Wilmington, DE: ISI, 2007.
Ritzer, George. *The McDonaldization of Society 5*. Thousand Oaks, CA: Pine Forge, 2008.
Rosen, Stanley. *Hermeneutics as Politics*. 2nd ed. New Haven, CT: Yale University Press, 2003.
———. *Nihilism: A Philosophical Essay*. South Bend, IN: St. Augustine's, 2000.
Rousseau, Jean-Jacques. *Rousseau: "The Discourses" and Other Early Political Writings*. Edited by Victor Gourevitch. Cambridge Texts in the History of Political Thought. New York: Cambridge University Press, 2008.
Ryken, Philip Graham. *City on a Hill: Reclaiming the Biblical Pattern for the Church in the 21st Century*. Chicago: Moody, 2003.

Ryle, J. C. *Luke 11–24.* Vol. 2 of *Ryle's Expository Thoughts on the Gospels.* Grand Rapids: Baker, 1977.
Sempangi, F. Kefa. *A Distant Grief.* Glendale, CA: Regal, G/L, 1979.
Simpson, E. K., and F. F. Bruce. *Commentary on the Epistles to the Ephesians and the Colossians.* NICNT. Grand Rapids: Eerdmans, 1979.
Smith, Christian, with Melinda Lundquist Denton. *Soul Searching: The Religious and Spiritual Lives of American Teenagers.* Oxford: Oxford University Press, 2005.
Sproul, R. C. "3 Types of Legalism." Ligonier, July 17, 2019. https://www.ligonier.org/learn/articles/3-types-legalism.
Stivers, Richard. *Shades of Loneliness: Pathologies of a Technological Society.* Lanham, MD: Rowman and Littlefield, 2004.
Stott, John R. W. *Christian Counter-Culture.* Downers Grove, IL: InterVarsity, 1978.
———. *Ephesians: Building a Community in Christ.* John Stott Bible Studies. Downers Grove, IL: IVP, 2008.
Taylor, Charles. *The Ethics of Authenticity.* Cambridge, MA: Harvard University Press, 1991.
———. *Hegel.* New York: Cambridge University Press, 1999.
———. *Philosophical Arguments.* Cambridge, MA: Harvard University Press, 1997.
———. *A Secular Age.* Cambridge, MA: Belknap, 2007.
———. *Sources of the Self: The Making of the Modern Identity.* Cambridge, MA: Harvard University Press, 1989.
Thomas, Robert L., ed. *New American Standard Exhaustive Concordance of the Bible.* Nashville: Holman, 1981.
Tocqueville, Alexis de. *Democracy in America.* Translated by Arthur Goldhammer. New York: Literary Classics of the United States, 2004.
———. *The Old Regime and the French Revolution.* Translated by Stuart Gilbert. New York: Doubleday, 1983.
Tripp, Paul David. *New Morning Mercies: A Daily Gospel Devotional.* Wheaton, IL: Crossway, 2014.
Trueman, Carl. "Courageous Protestantism? Some Reflections on David Wells's Analysis of the Contemporary Church: A Review Article." *Ordained Servant Online*, Apr. 2009. http://opc.org/os.html?article_id=147.
Unamuno, Miguel de. *Tragic Sense of Life.* Translated by J. E. Crawford Flitch. New York: Dover, 2012.
Wallace, David Foster. "This Is Water." Farnam Street, May 21, 2005. https://fs.blog/2012/04/david-foster-wallace-this-is-water/.
Wallis, R. T. *Neoplatonism.* Hackett Classics. Indianapolis: Hackett, 1995.
Warfield, Benjamin B. *Selected Shorter Writings of Benjamin B. Warfield.* Edited by John E. Meeter. 2 vols. Phillipsburg, NJ: Presbyterian and Reformed, 1980.
Wells, David F. *The Courage to Be Protestant: Truth-Lovers, Marketers, and Emergents in the Postmodern World.* Grand Rapids: Eerdmans, 2008.
———. *God in the Wasteland: The Reality of Truth in a World of Fading Dreams.* Grand Rapids: Eerdmans, 1994.
Westphal, Merold. *Kierkegaard's Critique of Reason and Society.* Macon: Mercer University Press, 1987.
———. "Kierkegaard's Sociology." In *Two Ages: The Present Age and the Age of Revolution; A Literary Review*, edited by Robert L. Perkins, 133–54. Vol. 14 of *International Kierkegaard Commentary.* Macon: Mercer University Press, 1984.

———. *Suspicion & Faith: The Religious Uses of Modern Atheism.* New York: Fordham University Press, 2009.
Whitehead, Alfred North. *Science and the Modern World.* New York: Free Press, 1967.
Winter, Nancy B., ed. *Heart of the Matter: Daily Reflections for Changing Hearts and Lives.* Greensboro, NC: New Growth, 2012.
Wittgenstein, Ludwig. *Philosophical Investigations.* Translated by G. E. M. Anscombe et al. 4th ed. N.p.: Sheridan, 2017.
Wuthnow, Robert. *The Crisis in the Churches: Spiritual Malaise, Fiscal Woe.* New York: Oxford University Press, 1997.

Author Index

Adorno, Theodor, 28, 143
Arendt, Hannah, xi, 27, 112, 143
Aristotle, 72, 94–96, 99–100, 104, 143
Augustine, 2, 8, 62, 141, 143

Baugh, Stephen M., 89n2, 143
Bavinck, Herman, 118n11, 128, 143
Bellah, Robert N., 30–36, 143
Berlin, Isaiah, 6, 143
Brown, John, 110, 143
Bruce, F. F., 134, 148
Buber, Martin, 113, 143

Calvin, John, 10n23, 62, 85–86, 96, 98, 111, 116, 117, 125, 129, 143
Candlish, Robert S., 61n1, 143
Coleridge, Samuel Taylor, 13, 143
Constant, Benjamin, 35, 36n28, 144
Cragg, G. R., 113, 144

Denton, Melinda Lundquist, 51n10, 144
Descartes, Rene, 59, 70–72, 73n13, 74–76, 78–79, 107, 115, 119, 144
Dieleman, Karen, 69, 144
Dreyfus, Hubert, 70n2, 73n11, 73n14, 74n15, 144
Dumont, Louis, 30, 31n7, 144
Dupré, Louis, 81n15, 144

Farnsworth, Hal, 54n19, 144
Ferry, Luc, 50, 144
Frame, John M., 117n10, 144

Furedi, Frank, 20, 41, 43–44, 144

Gadamer, Hans-Georg, 122, 144
Gaffin, Richard B., Jr., 126n3, 127, 133–34, 144
Gardner, Stephen L., 32n17, 144
Gauchet, Marcel, 42–44, 144
Gillespie, Michael Allen, 70, 72, 144
Goethe, Johann Wolfgang von, 46, 144
Goldwin, Robert A., 28n46, 144
Guinness, Os, 57, 115, 118, 145

Hart, David Bentley, 8–9, 145
Hayek, F. A., 125, 145
Hegel, G. W. F., 24, 112–13, 127n8–9, 145, 148
Heidegger, Martin, 6n11, 9, 25n31, 64, 67, 75, 84, 96n4, 104–7, 109, 137, 145
Helm, Paul, 11–12, 76, 77n22–23, 145
Hendriksen, William, 108–10, 129, 143, 145
Hodge, Charles, 63, 88, 110, 145
Horkheimer, Max, 12, 145
Huxley, Aldous, 41–42, 145

Ihde, Don, 21n69, 74n16, 145
Illouz, Eva, 21, 128, 145

Jacobi, Friedrich Heinrich, 115n3, 145
Jacobs, Alan, 34n22, 145
Jaspers, Karl, 27, 49, 53, 128n15, 146

AUTHOR INDEX

Kierkegaard, Søren, vi–vii, ix, xi, 9, 10n21, 13, 14n27, 22, 49n1, 50, 51n11, 53, 76, 79–85, 98, 113, 120, 127, 128n11, 144, 146, 148

Levinas, Emmanuel, 62n5, 74, 75n17, 146
Lloyd-Jones, Martyn, 49n2, 146
Luther, Martin, 57, 80, 110, 117, 146

Machen, J. Gresham, 52, 63, 84, 117n10, 128–29, 144, 146
MacIntyre, Alasdair, 50, 146
Macpherson, C. B., 28n47, 146
Manent, Pierre, 135–36, 146
Merleau-Ponty, Maurice, vi, 72, 73n12, 80, 119n13–14, 132, 146
More, Robert, Jr., 9n18, 146
Moskowitz, Eva S., 21, 46, 47, 146
Murdoch, Iris, 131, 147
Murray, John J., 9, 147

Nietzsche, Friedrich, vi–vii, 27, 33, 38, 70n1, 72n9, 79, 84–85, 137, 144, 147
Noll, Mark A., 25n31, 62n3, 120, 147

Oakeshott, Michael, 120–21, 147
Ortega y Gasset, José, 6n9, 119, 147

Packer, J. I., 100–1, 147
Pascal, Blaise, 64, 147
Piper, John, 46n23, 147
Plato, 6, 11n23, 94, 96–97, 99n18, 105–7, 115, 130, 145, 147
Plotinus, 62, 71, 78, 147
Plumer, William S., 102n24, 147

Rehnman, Sebastian, 4, 147
Ridderbos, Herman, 62, 126, 147

Rieff, Philip, 28, 38–42, 45n20, 47, 57, 147
Ritzer, George, 49, 147
Rosen, Stanley, 7n12, 121, 147
Rousseau, Jean-Jacques, 50, 147
Ryken, Philip Graham, 66n14, 147
Ryle, J. C., 82, 83n19, 148

Sempangi, F. Kefa, 123–24, 148
Simpson, E. K., 134n11, 148
Smith, Christian, 51n10, 148
Sproul, R. C., 8, 45, 148
Stivers, Richard, 34n23, 148
Stott, John R. W., 54, 134, 148

Taylor, Charles, 20, 27, 36n31, 70n2, 73n11, 73n13–14, 74n15, 76–78, 120n17, 126–27, 133, 144, 148
Thomas, Robert L., 108n12, 148
Tocqueville, Alexis de, 17–27, 30–31, 34–35, 39, 44, 53, 55n21, 71, 81n14, 92, 148
Tripp, Paul David, 51n9, 67, 82, 91, 148
Trueman, Carl, 3, 4n6, 126, 136n15, 148

Unamuno, Miguel de, 64, 148

Wallace, David Foster, 57, 148
Wallis, R. T., 62, 71n3–4, 148
Warfield, Benjamin B., 1, 13, 148
Wells, David F., 3, 10, 37, 48, 52–54, 117n9, 126n4, 128, 148
Westphal, Merold, 53n18, 78n27, 98n12, 148
Whitehead, Alfred North, 85, 149
Winter, Nancy B., 128n13, 149
Wittgenstein, Ludwig, vi, 6, 66, 82, 149
Wuthnow, Robert, 34, 133n7, 149

Subject Index

abstraction, 24, 74, 80, 92, 112, 115, 118–20, 122–24, 127, 133n5
aesthete/aesthetic, 4, 23, 26, 32–34, 37, 41, 43, 45, 47, 50–52, 54–56, 63, 82–83, 85, 90, 94, 101–2, 120, 124
aletheia, 7, 89n2, 103–9, 111–12

biblespeak, 10, 28, 35, 55, 120
body, vi, 7–8, 10, 21, 31, 35–36, 44, 56, 67, 69, 71–72, 74–76, 78, 88–89, 91–92, 95, 98, 100, 103, 108–9, 111n21, 112, 114, 119, 128, 132–33, 135–37
bourgeois, 5, 28, 45, 65
buffered self, 20, 77–78

Cartesian, vii, 5, 7–8, 44, 47, 62, 65, 68–79, 81, 86–88, 90–92, 95, 100, 103–4, 112–14, 119, 126, 133
cheap grace, 48
cogito, 70–71, 79n1, 112
communal, 35, 38–42, 44, 77
consciousness, vii, 2, 5–6, 8, 11, 17, 44, 47, 62, 64–65, 68–70, 73, 75, 77, 79, 81, 83–84, 87, 91–92, 95, 100, 104–5, 107, 114, 119

democracy, vii, xi, 2, 7, 17, 18n4, 20–24, 30, 38–39, 49, 81n14, 135
disengagement, 7, 70–71, 76–78
duties, 6, 13, 23, 33, 46, 49, 77–78, 98–99, 109, 131, 133, 135–37,

easy-believism, 48–49, 51–53, 55–56, 77
egoism, 18–19, 37, 39
embodied/embody, 83, 103, 107, 109–113, 128
Enlightenment, 127, 133
equality, vii, 2, 7, 17–22, 24–26, 36, 39, 49, 120
existential, ix–x, 2, 7–8, 10, 14n27, 28, 43, 45, 47, 51, 63, 70, 80, 83, 89–90, 94, 98, 101–2, 107, 114, 116, 119, 123–24, 129, 133, 137

fruit, 43, 61, 90–92, 110–11, 128–29

Gnosticism, 6, 56, 69, 73, 76
godtalk, 55, 81, 120
good works, 46, 61, 109–110, 125, 129, 133, 134n11

heart, vii, 6–7, 13, 18–19, 24, 30, 54–55, 62–65, 75, 80, 83, 86, 87–95, 102–3, 107, 111n20, 112, 129, 132
herd, 53, 55, 85

individualism, x, 2–3, 5, 17–25, 27–40, 42, 44, 49, 53, 56, 121
intellectualism, 5, 8, 12, 44, 52, 54, 62–66, 68–69, 71, 114, 118, 121n23, 123–24, 127

legalism, 45
leveling, 53–54

SUBJECT INDEX

neighbor, x–xi, 2–3, 5, 7–8, 12–13, 19, 21–25, 28, 31, 34–36, 38–40, 44–46, 53–54, 63, 65n, 66, 68, 74–77, 83–86, 99, 114, 118–19, 127, 129n17, 132–33, 135–41
Neoplatonism, 78
nihilism, 32–33, 42, 44, 137

orthodoxy, 53, 64, 67, 69, 75, 82–84, 116

paganism, 1, 4–5, 11, 37, 81, 105
pathos, 83–84
populism, 24, 48–49, 51–53, 55

rationalism, 72, 74–76, 115, 120, 128, 130
reason, 1, 3, 9–12, 24, 27–28, 39, 63–64, 71, 73, 75–77, 87–88, 99, 115, 117n9, 118–19, 128
run, 19, 21, 46, 68, 99, 102, 104, 110, 139–41

system, vii, 3, 39, 42–44, 55, 57, 62, 64, 67, 80, 104, 113–22, 124–26, 128–29, 131–32, 135, 137
subjectivity, vii, 28, 31–32, 79–81, 83, 90, 107

technology, 41, 135
theology, vii, 4, 6–7, 10, 12, 24, 28, 36, 47–49, 52–55, 62–63, 74, 78, 86, 88, 98, 100–101, 114, 116–19, 124–25, 126n3, 127–28, 130
theological correctness, 45, 63, 75–76, 87, 92, 102, 104, 120
therapeutic, vii, 5, 7, 20–21, 32, 34–36, 38–47, 51, 74, 85

unconcealing, 102, 104, 106, 108–111

walk, 3–4, 21, 43, 61, 64, 75, 90, 97–98, 109, 128–29, 133, 140–41

www.ingramcontent.com/pod-product-compliance
Lightning Source LLC
Chambersburg PA
CBHW060820190426
43197CB00038B/2166